Published by:
The Royal Zoological Society of
Scotland
Murrayfield
EDINBURGH EH12 6TS
Telephone: 031-334 9171

Produced and co-ordinated by:
Fiona Pringle
Text by:
Robert J Ollason
Edited by:
Miranda Stevenson
Contributors:
Professor David Bellamy,
BSc, PhD, FLS
David Taylor, BVMS, FRCVS

Designed by:
McIlroy Coates
Typeset by:
Artwork Associates
Artwork by:
George Studios
Colour separations by:
Transcolour
Printed by:
Alna Press Ltd
Printed on
Success Extra Art, 115 gms,
from Hafrestrom AB from
Wiggins Teape Paper

Colour photography by:
Cedric Martin
Film sponsored by:
Kodak (UK) Ltd
Photographic acknowledgments
also to:
International Centre for
Conservation Education,
Ian R Thomson, Edwin Blake,
Miranda Stevenson,
David Houston, William Paton,
Douglas Sherriff,
Tom Scott Roxburgh,
Chris W Morris, Glasgow Herald

The Royal Zoological Society of
Scotland

Published to commemorate
Edinburgh Zoo's 75th Anniversary:
1988

Contents

The biggest colony of daily readers in Lothian

If it's in the news, it's in the News.

How do you teach your children the value of money and the importance of saving?

TSB makes it easy.

We've got two real bank accounts for children — Magic Bank for under 7's and Magic Micro Club for over 7's. Both accounts not only pay interest so your children can see their money grow, but because they're fun, also encourage children to save.

And when your children join Magic Bank or Magic Micro Club, each child receives a super free gift pack. (See above for details).

Why not call into your nearest TSB and open an account for your children that's really magic.

 MORE AND MORE YOUNG PEOPLE ARE SAYING _YES_

CATCH OUR JUMBOS AT THE AIRPORT. B·A·A Edinburgh

Get there by train.

No one spans the length and breadth of the country quite like ScotRail.

The coast, countryside and historic towns are all within easy reach by train and our services make the journey easy.

Save money, too, with Saver tickets or Railcards — and during the summer, our Days Out and Rover tickets are perfect for those breaks away with the family.

Pick up a free ScotRail timetable today — or ask for details of fares and services at mainline stations or rail appointed travel agents.

 ScotRail

EDINBURGH
· CRYSTAL ·

See the Crystal Glassmakers
at Edinburgh Crystal Visitors Centre

Witness the age old art of glassmaking at Edinburgh Crystal. Our Centre is open throughout the year Monday to Saturday, (Sundays – April to September incl.). Guided factory tours, which unveil every aspect of the glassmakers' craft are available Monday to Friday. Choose from a vast selection of 1st and 2nd quality crystal giftware and tableware in our large factory shop.

PETER ANDERSON of SCOTLAND operate an exclusive Woollen Mill Shop within the Centre.* Sample traditional Scottish fayre in the spacious Pentland View Licensed Restaurant (approved member "Taste of Scotland" scheme 1988). Picnic and children's play areas are provided and there is ample free parking for cars and coaches.

Glass Blowing

Glass Shearing

Glass Cutting

COLOROLL

EDINBURGH CRYSTAL DIVISION

For further information regarding opening times, holidays etc., please refer to Visitors Centre Information Leaflet or contact:

The Tours Organiser,
Edinburgh Crystal, Visitors Centre,
Eastfield Industrial Estate, Penicuik, Midlothian, EH26 8HB
Tel. No. (0968) 75128.

N.B. The PETER ANDERSON of SCOTLAND Woollen Mill Shop opens mid-May 1988 (Provisional)

Foreword

Welcome to Edinburgh Zoo, Scotland's largest animal collection. The Zoo is owned by the Royal Zoological Society of Scotland which is an educational and scientific charity that receives only limited financial assistance from public funds. It thus relies very largely on its membership and on the support given by visitors to the Park.

We have made a special effort in this our 75th Anniversary Commemorative Guidebook to update and inform you of all the fascinating animals and aspects of Edinburgh Zoo. It is intended as an invaluable guide to our Park and one I am sure you will wish to treasure and keep. I would like to thank all the people who have been involved in supporting, compiling and producing such a beautiful record of a park that has continued to develop and improve over the years.

The book will also guide you through the varied roles of the Zoo in conservation, education, research and entertainment. It will illustrate how the Zoo plays an important part in the survival of species and the instruction of both young and old alike, to reach a better understanding of animals.

The Zoo itself is like a book brought to life by an array of memorable characters and rich rewarding achievements. We hope that you will get as much pleasure from the pages of this guide as we experienced in the recording of such an historic chapter in the life and work of the Royal Zoological Society of Scotland.

I hope that you enjoy your visit to Edinburgh Zoo and will wish to come back again soon.

The Right Hon. The Viscount of Arbuthnott CBE, DSC, MA, FRSE
President of the Royal Zoological Society of Scotland

"Good Zoos Are Good News"

My first introduction to the living world of animals was a childhood trip to the Zoo, a trip which became a regular and eagerly awaited event. I queued to ride on the camel and elephant, ooh-aahd at the new arrivals, laughed with the antics at the Chimps' tea party, and had my photo taken with one of the partygoers. I also spent a lot of time watching the less glamorous members of the zoo community sitting alone in their cages and on the way home harried my parents, uncles and aunts about the rights and wrongs of captivity.

Since that time I have had the immense good fortune of travelling the world, of visiting its game reserves and national parks, and of seeing many of those animals in the wild. Each new experience has been a source of immense inspiration, and each has again made me question the ethics of captivity.

During that time I have also witnessed the mass destruction of the world's habitats and slaughter of wildlife on a scale too horrible to comprehend. In response to these obscene acts of vandalism the attitudes of all thinking people are changing and so are our zoos. Many keep one of their old Victorian cages, using it as a special exhibit, simply labelled "The World's Most Dangerous Animal", its contents a large mirror, a reflection of the reader.

Yes, zoos have taken on new and vital roles. They are places of refuge for a number of endangered species, a living genetic bank from which, when the world comes to its senses, we may be able to repopulate areas with descendants of the animals which originally lived there. Active research and international zoo co-operation is ensuring diversification of the gene-stock and providing more compatible conditions in which the animals live a more challenging life and will increase in number.

They are also places of education where children and adults can face the real facts of caring, sharing and of survival, for I know that we cannot survive alone on this planet – we must share it with all the other animals and plants.

Good zoos are good news, and Edinburgh is one of them. Please, please come, and come often; marvel at the wonder of the animals and the stupidity of those humans who will destroy anything for the sake of personal gain. Give the Zoo and its workers your support and work with them to improve the lot of all animals in captivity and hope for all those in the wild.

Thank You for Caring.

DAVID J BELLAMY

PS 28 Penguin Chicks Can't Be Wrong

A National Zoo for Scotland

'To promote, facilitate and encourage the study of Zoology and kindred subjects and to foster and develop among the people an interest in and a knowledge of animal life'.

Charter of the Royal Zoological Society of Scotland

From the formation of the Royal Zoological Society of Scotland in 1909, it took Thomas Gillespie four years to establish his "Zoo for Scotland" before its public opening on 22nd July 1913. Gillespie's inspiration for Edinburgh Zoo, came not from the meagre Victorian menageries prevalent at that time, but from the work of a German, Carl Hagenbeck, who had built Hamburg Zoo. The principle was an 'Open Zoo' with limited use of bars and, instead, large natural enclosures that employed ditches and moats to separate the animals from the public.

Gillespie writes that the opening of the zoo was "the triumphant fulfilment of

more than four years of hope, frustration and effort". He goes on to document the pandemonium of the last few days before its historic opening, with many enclosures not ready and the last-minute loan of many animals from a private collector in Kent. However, misgivings about opening slightly unprepared were soon swept aside as the crowds flocked in such considerable numbers as to leave the Society in no doubt of the Zoo's future success. This success has scarcely waned throughout the Zoo's history despite two world wars that caused great hardships from bombings and food shortages.

It was the arrival of three Antarctic king penguins from a Christian Salvesen Whaling expedition in January 1914 and the subsequent first successful hatching of a young king penguin chick in 1919 that made the Zoo "famous all over the world". For these were the first penguins ever seen outside their Antarctic homeland. The colony of penguins, that resulted from Salvesen's continuing interest and donations, has since become the crowning glory of the park.

Through the ages the Zoo has pioneered much in the fields of research, breeding programmes and, in particular, education. It has attained a number of breeding achievements and longevity records and it has always maintained a gallery of fascinating stars and personal favourites such as Spot the elephant seal, Mickey the largest-ever

orang utan, Philip the chimpanzee and Sally the elephant.

The Zoo has always concentrated on improving and developing the Park. In the last twelve years many of the enclosures have been redesigned or extended including the Chimpanzee Exhibit, the Giraffe Enclosure and the Big Cats' Rock Dens. In 1973, the Education Centre opened and has established an international reputation. The Orientation and Entrance Centre,

being developed at the time of writing, is also a pioneering venture for a British Zoo and is intended to increase the public's understanding and enjoyment of their visit.

Thomas Gillespie would be proud to know that, 75 years on, his 'hope, frustration and effort' have been so well rewarded and respected. The Zoo may have travelled a long way from its early years but its foundation promise to "foster and develop among the people an interest in and a knowledge of animal life" will never alter.

The Role of the Zoo Today

Edinburgh Zoo is at the forefront in achieving the goals of today's most progressive and forward-thinking zoos. We are strongly on course in advancing our objectives relating to conservation of wildlife, education and research, as well as recreation for the general visitor.

On one of the most naturally beautiful zoo sites in the world, Edinburgh Zoo strives, within its limited budget, to exhibit animals in ways which take account both of the species' natural habits and lifestyles, and of the public's attitude to animals "behind bars". For the visitors, we aim to create an illusion of freedom with, where possible, a reduction in the use of visual barriers. For the animals, every effort is made to ensure that the captive environment includes the optimum space and accommodation for the numbers of individuals necessary to natural courtship and reproductive behaviour,

and the rearing of young. In addition, enclosures, where applicable, are furnished with facilities enabling the animals to engage in climbing, burrowing and swimming, exploring and playing. Only by perceiving the animals in some replication of their wild state, can the visitor be expected to feel concern about them and their plight in the wild. Such captive animals are ambassadors for their kind, still in the wild. It is through them that we hope to raise public awareness of the urgent need for conservation, not only of the world's remaining wild animals, but also of its wild places.

Like other zoos of its calibre, Edinburgh has long since shed the label of "consumers" of wildlife and is now, most certainly, one of the "producers" of animals, contributing substantially to the captive banks of many endangered species and others, less rare. Edinburgh Zoo is a highly active member of the Federation of Zoos of Britain and Ireland and, through the Society's Director, of the International Union of Directors of Zoological Gardens. The Zoo is fully involved in both national and international exchange of animals, captive breeding programmes and the computerisation, both in this country and abroad, of many of our animal records and information. The following pages give some idea of our commitment to conservation within zoos, and the part we play in its international aspect.

Closely linked to conservation, is education and Edinburgh Zoo's Education Department is one of Britain's largest and most effective, both in formal programmes for school pupils, and in informal educational experiences for the general visitor. The activities of the Education Department are dealt with more fully on Pages 98 and 99.

In the field of research, Edinburgh Zoo allows its animals to be the subjects of non-invasive projects by university students. We have a research post in the Zoo for a student of animal behaviour, funded by the Manpower Services Commission and, to date, studies have been undertaken on our red pandas, penguins and gorillas. By further increasing our knowledge in respect of these species, we are better able to improve the animals' environments and their breeding prospects.

Primates

Apes and monkeys belong to the group of mammals which includes man – the primates. We have many features in common, one of which is a large brain. Other shared features are the grasping hand – an adaptation to living in trees – and the fact that our eyes are "forward-facing", enabling us to judge distance. Also classified as primates, are animals such as lemurs, bush-babies and lorises. Most primates, other than man, lead a tree-based life in tropical parts of the world.

Apes

Gorillas, chimpanzees, orang utans and gibbons are all apes. In general they are larger than monkeys and have no tails. Their arms are longer than their legs, allowing them to swing along underneath branches – we call this "brachiation".

On the ground, gorillas and chimpanzees "knuckle-walk" and gibbons run for short distances on their hind legs, balancing themselves with outstretched arms.

Siamang

Siamangs are the largest species of gibbon and gibbons are the smallest of the apes. Gibbons are the aerial acrobats of the forest canopies, aided by their light bodies and long arms and fingers. In the wild, gibbons live in family groups and keep others at a distance from their territories by issuing loud, hooting calls. The calls of the siamang are particularly penetrating, due to an inflatable throat-sack which increases the volume of sound.

Our female siamang from Twycross Zoo took some time to accept and adjust to the male, which arrived from Boston Zoo in the United States, early in 1987. Now they are interacting normally and their calls, echoing round the Zoo, create an exotic atmosphere, especially in the early mornings.

The species is endangered due to deforestation of its wild habitat in Malaysia and Sumatra, and hopefully, in the near future, Edinburgh Zoo will contribute to its breeding in captivity.

Chimpanzee

In Africa, wild chimpanzees are social animals, living in loosely-connected groups, composed of several males, females and offspring of various ages. They spend time on the ground as well as in the trees, and are excitable and noisy animals. Sticks and leaves are used as "tools" to help them forage and drink.

Edinburgh Zoo's group of chimpanzees usually numbers about a dozen animals, ranging in age from males over thirty to infants. Breeding occurs regularly and the spacious enclosure and varied climbing "furniture" encourage natural behaviour amongst the individuals.

As in the wild, their daily life here includes periods of non-serious squabbling, when their shrieks and "tantrums" can be heard all over the Zoo.

Fortunately chimpanzee tea parties are an event of the past in most zoos. Chimps are fascinating in their own right and do not need to copy humans in order to be interesting. Watch them at their fake termite mound. In the wild they poke twigs into holes in the mounds and "fish" for termites and ants. Here in the Zoo they "fish" through the holes for honey, concealed inside the mound.

Chimpanzees breed quite well in captivity these days and, with national and international exchange of animals for breeding programmes, no reputable zoo would encourage, or indeed consider necessary, the taking of animals from the wild.

MAP
32
LOCATION

Western Lowland Gorilla

Surpassing the other apes, and also man, in size, the gorilla is the largest primate. Gorillas are severely threatened in their diminishing forested strongholds in West and Central Africa, due to human encroachment and hunting. Three sub-species of gorilla are recognised – the eastern and western lowland gorilla and the mountain gorilla. The latter now numbers only about 400 individuals in the wild. The western lowland gorilla is the one most commonly kept in zoos. These "gentle giants" live life at a leisurely pace in shrinking pockets of forest, where small troops are led by adult males known as "silver-backs".

Although gorillas are tree climbers like other apes, adult males spend much time on the ground due to their great weight.

The first gorillas to be seen in Scotland arrived in Edinburgh Zoo during the summer of 1985. In July, from Rotterdam Zoo, came a splendid silver-back male aged thirteen years. Several days later he was joined by an eight year-old female from Bristol Zoo, and at the end of the summer, by a second female, aged thirteen years, from Dublin Zoo. The trio settled down well together and in late 1986 the chances of breeding were increased by the acquisition of another adult male.

For several years now, responsible zoos have agreed a voluntary ban on taking gorillas from the wild, and have put all their efforts into captive breeding. Our gorillas do not actually belong to Edinburgh Zoo and will not necessarily spend their entire lives here. They form part of the breeding programme of the zoos of Britain and Ireland. The Anthropoid Ape Advisory Panel, which is chaired by Edinburgh Zoo's director, monitors and recommends movement of the animals within this programme, to maximise the breeding potential nationwide.

Ring-Tailed Lemur and White-Fronted Lemur

There are over twenty species of lemur, varying greatly in size, and all unique to the island of Madagascar, where they have evolved in isolation for millions of years. They are not monkeys – only related to them – and are known as the prosimians. Their future in Madagascar is now very uncertain, due to deforestation making way for crop plantations and other developments, and general lack of conservation.

For some years we have exhibited and bred the least endangered species, and the one most commonly seen in zoos – the ring-tailed lemur. We now also have a breeding trio of the white-fronted lemur. Both species are on show in the Monkey House.

Monkeys

There are over 130 species of monkey and, like apes, they are adapted to life in trees. Unlike apes, monkeys run along the tops of branches and leap from one branch or tree to another. Apart from some species of macaque monkey, they all live in the warmer parts of the world. Those that live in Africa or Asia are known as the Old World monkeys, and those that inhabit Central and South America are the New World monkeys. Only the douroucouli or owl monkey from South America is nocturnal; all the others are active during daytime, and all are social animals, living in troops or family groups.

Old World Monkeys

Unlike their relatives in the New World, these monkeys have downward-pointing nostrils and tough pads underneath their tails on which to sit whilst sleeping. Included in this group are the successful and wide-ranging baboons and macaque monkeys, which, to a certain extent, have adapted to life on the ground.

You can see breeding groups of Old World monkeys in the main Monkey House, the adjacent enclosure for stump-tailed macaques and the Barbary Macaque Rock.

Barbary Macaque

These so-called Barbary or Gibraltar "apes" are not apes at all, but monkeys with no tails. A small number do live wild on Gibraltar, descendants of a group introduced from North Africa in 1740. Legend has it that Gibraltar will stay under British rule only as long as the monkeys remain there, so, when their numbers dropped to only four in 1943, Winston Churchill immediately ordered more to be brought over from Morocco! The group is now stable at 30-40 monkeys.

Our small family group has a spacious range on the Zoo's former Baboon Rock, and, as this species is adaptable to cooler regions, the monkeys are not shut in at night.

MAP LOCATION 59

Stump-Tailed Macaque

Alongside the Monkey House is the Stump-tailed Macaque Enclosure. A plaque on its wall explains the rather interesting story behind the construction of this exhibit.

These Asian monkeys are adapted to life on the ground as well as in the trees. Watch them search for the grain which we mix with the gravel in their enclosure – the time taken to do this prevents them from becoming bored.

De Brazza Monkey

This very striking monkey belongs to the guenon family and is found in forested parts of Africa, where, due to habitat destruction, its numbers are now declining. This is one of the few monkey species we exhibit which, so far, (February 1988) has not yet bred, and we may have to bring in individuals from other zoos in order to achieve success. Like most of our monkeys, the De Brazzas receive small portions of cooked chicken each week to supplement their otherwise vegetarian diet.

Diana Monkey

Also from Africa, the forest-living Diana monkeys have excellent colour vision. Their distinctive markings, both front and rear, help them to recognise their own kind even amongst dense foliage. This applies also to the De Brazza monkey.

Our Diana monkeys have bred regularly over the past few years. Edinburgh Zoo is the Regional Studbook keeper for this species and enters on computer the records and information pertaining to all the Diana monkeys in British and Irish zoos.

Dusky or Spectacled Langur

Langurs are leaf-eaters from Asia. They are difficult to keep in captivity unless they will accept a "substitute" diet which, in addition to leaves and branches, includes lettuce, banana, carrot, apple and tomato. We have bred them several times. The young are bright orange-coloured for the first few months of their lives, possibly as an aid to recognition by other members of the troop.

New World Monkeys

The monkeys of Central and South America differ from those of the Old World in a number of ways – in the formation of their noses and in the shape and number of their teeth. Only in New World monkeys do we find prehensile tails and, as a rule, the young of New World monkeys are carried on the back, whereas those of Old World monkeys are carried on the chest.

Our New World monkeys can be seen in the Monkey House and in the Marmoset Complex, opposite the Chimpanzee Exhibit.

White-Faced Saki Monkey

The males and females of this unusual species from northern South America look very different from each other. Males are very black with white mask-like faces, whilst the females are much greyer with subtly-marked faces. Notice how the fur in both sexes is unusual because of the downward direction in which it grows.

We have had considerable success since introducing this species to the Zoo a few years ago. Our first infant had to be hand-reared, but, as this was done without loss of contact with his parents, it was possible, after weaning, to reintroduce him to them. Now, as an adult, he has a mate of his own and we hope they will breed. This species tends to live in pairs with their offspring, rather than in troops.

Black-Capped Capuchin Monkey

This South American species has a partly-prehensile tail which can wrap round branches to give the animal extra support and balance when feeding or reaching for food. Only when the monkey is very young can the tail take the animal's entire weight, and then only for a short period of time.

Like other monkeys, the capuchins will groom their own and each other's fur with the utmost care and patience, removing any pieces of dandruff or grit and, often, eating it. During this activity, a great sense of wellbeing is evident in the monkeys, whether they are grooming or being groomed. This no doubt cements bonds within the group and helps keep aggression to a minimum.

Marmosets and Tamarins

The smallest monkeys in the world are the marmosets and tamarins which inhabit the forests of South America. They usually give birth to twins which are carried round on the backs of various members of the group, then handed back to the mother for feeding. Normally only the dominant females in a group will breed. Marmosets are gum feeders, their specialised dentition enabling them to gnaw branches from which the gum flows.

Common Marmoset

These were the first marmosets to be acquired by Edinburgh Zoo and they share an exhibit in the Monkey House with acouchis – South American rodents. We have bred the marmosets many times, exchanging individuals with other zoos to keep the gene pool as wide as possible. Infants can often be seen clinging to the backs of adults in the troop, but they are difficult to spot as they blend perfectly with the adults' fur.

All our other species of marmoset and tamarin are housed in the Marmoset Complex, opposite the Chimpanzee Exhibit.

(MAP 20 LOCATION)

Tamarins

Tamarins on show and, in some cases, breeding, are the cotton-top tamarin (right), red-bellied tamarin, red-handed tamarin and Goeldi's monkey (left).

Many of these smaller monkeys are rare and some are highly endangered. The main threat to their survival is deforestation as more demands are made for agricultural development. Some are hunted and others captured for research. Fragmented pockets of forest are being created, thus isolating populations of certain species. Their conservation is of utmost importance in the zoo world; several zoos are engaged in breeding and reintroduction programmes involving the golden lion tamarin.

(MAP 36 LOCATION)

Pygmy Marmoset ▲

Tiniest of all the marmosets and tamarins and, therefore, the smallest primate, pygmy marmosets are well-camouflaged against branches and one has to look hard to see them. An adult can fit into a teacup. They have bred well here and we believe we have a zoo "first" – mother-reared triplets in 1986.

(MAP 36 LOCATION)

The Big Cats

The cat family includes more than 35 species, ranging in size from the domestic cat to the Siberian tiger. All are strictly carnivorous and they are highly efficient and deadly hunters. Most cats share several features – keen senses, short strong jaws, specialised teeth for killing and sharp claws – but six of the larger ones possess the ability to roar and they are often referred to as the "big cats". They are the lion, tiger, jaguar, leopard, snow leopard and clouded leopard.

African Lion

African lions, despite their range being greatly diminished, are not endangered animals and they breed well in captivity, whether it be in zoos, safari parks or even circuses.

Lions have always been exhibited at Edinburgh Zoo and we have raised many cubs over the years. In order to ensure that we do not have cubs too frequently and are able to place them in other zoos, our current lioness has a contraceptive device implanted in her shoulder.

Our Lion Rock dates from 1913 and is one of the two oldest permanent exhibits in the Zoo. Despite its age, it is very modern in concept – the lions being restrained behind a cleverly concealed ditch.

MAP LOCATION 58

Siberian Tiger

For many years Edinburgh Zoo was famous for breeding Bengal tigers, but in 1984 decided to change to the largest race of tiger – the Siberian tiger. Less than 200 remain in the wild and just over 1000 are registered in the world's zoos. We acquired a pure-bred Siberian tigress from Marwell Zoo, and Leipzig Zoo, which keeps the studbook of Siberian tigers, suggested we bring a male from Minnesota Zoo to introduce a new blood line into the breeding programme. Our first two cubs are now in Amsterdam Zoo and a French zoo, and a second litter of three cubs was born in September 1986. Two of these are now in English zoos.

Like our lioness, our tigress is also temporarily fitted with a contraceptive device, ensuring that, in conjunction with other zoos, the breeding of Siberian tigers is planned to take account of needs, rather than occurring haphazardly and creating a surplus of unwanted cubs.

MAP LOCATION 69

Persian Leopard

In 1987 the Zoo received a pair of the rare Persian leopards, the male from an English zoo and the female from Adelaide Zoo in Australia. Again the idea was to mix two totally unrelated captive-bred animals, so that we might maximise the chances of successful breeding and healthy offspring, as it is important to raise the population of this species in zoos. The animals are housed in the newly refurbished Rock Dens, but have taken some time to settle, due to the disturbance caused by continuing work on adjacent enclosures.

They differ from the African leopards in having a very pale coat colour and light aquamarine eyes.

MAP LOCATION 68

Snow Leopard

The animals to occupy the first of our new Rock Dens were a pair of snow leopards from Marwell Zoo. This species is seriously endangered in the foothills of the Himalayas and surrounding mountains, but is breeding well in a number of zoos. As is the case with all the cats housed in the Rock Dens, they have completely private cubbing quarters hidden behind the rear of the exhibit and we hope that we, too, will be breeding them before long.

The animals are under pressure in the wild for their luxurious fur, which both insulates them superbly and camouflages them against the rocky scree of their habitat. In the Zoo they are also camouflaged against the stone backdrop to the exhibit and visitors sometimes assume they are not on view.

MAP LOCATION 68

Jaguar

Our pair of jaguars have so far reared four sets of twins – all of which are now in other zoos. When our female has cubs, the male is always separated from her. As lions are the only truly social cats, they are the only species which, in the wild, tolerates the presence of males during cub-rearing. In zoos, this is not necessarily so, and depending on the nature of individual animals, certain cats such as tigers and snow leopards are quite often exhibited as family groups. Our male tiger shows great tolerance of his offspring.

Some visitors find it difficult to distinguish between jaguars and leopards. Apart from some differences which are not easy to recognise, the "rosettes" on a jaguar's sides are usually heavier and bolder than those of a leopard, and often contain one or two central dark spots – which never occur within the rosettes on a leopard's coat.

MAP LOCATION 68

With the exception of lions, the other big cats have all suffered drastic reductions in their numbers due to man's desire for their skins. Protection laws exist, but poaching still goes on. In more recent years, the greatest threat, particularly to tigers, is the destruction of habitat, although India has done much to set aside conservation areas where the tigers' habitat and prey are protected. The Indian lion is, of course, endangered and exists only in the Gir Forest in Western India.

Smaller Cats

Equally as efficient hunters as the "big cats", smaller cats are found in a variety of habitats throughout most of the world except Australia. Many of the species are similar to one another, and several of them, like their larger relatives, are declining in numbers, due to the demand for their fur and to deforestation.

The Small Carnivore Complex, adjoining the Brown Bear Rock, will open in the early summer of 1988, housing, initially, margays, leopard cats and bush dogs. Eventually, pygmy mongooses may replace the leopard cats.

Margay

Very similar to the better-known ocelot, the margay is also found in South American forests. They are exceptionally agile climbers and are thought to hunt almost solely in the trees. Like the ocelot, the margay is hunted for its fur – in fact margay pelts are often sold as the more expensive ocelot skins. As yet, we have had no success in breeding our margays.

MAP LOCATION 54

Jungle Cat

Widely distributed in Asia, but mainly limited to the Nile Delta in Africa, the jungle cat or reed cat was used by the ancient Egyptians to hunt wildfowl. It inhabits swampy forests and impenetrable, marshy reed-beds. Note the longish legs and short tail. Our jungle cats have bred but the kittens did not survive.

MAP LOCATION 51

European Wildcat ▶

Housed opposite the Barbary Macaque Rock are the European wildcats which, in Britain, are now found only in parts of Scotland. Unfortunately, they will interbreed with feral domestic cats, but a true wildcat should have a sturdy build, a flattish skull and a squared-off tip to its black-ringed tail. It is our intention to breed wildcats in the Highland Wildlife Park only, in the future, and the Zoo exhibit will be redesigned to accommodate jungle cats.

Leopard Cat

This attractively-marked and aptly-named small cat from South East Asian forests has bred well at Edinburgh Zoo and a number of litters have been reared. We are most encouraged by this, as small cats in general are very sensitive to disturbance and are often difficult to breed in captivity. Unfortunately for the visitor, this species tends to be active at night, and, during the day, more often than not, is curled up in a hollow log.

Siberian Lynx ▼

Lynx are medium-sized cats of the northern hemisphere with longish legs, short tails and tufted ears. Their luxuriant fur is much prized and the fur trade contributes substantially to their decline in numbers. The Zoo has recently acquired a pair of the Siberian sub-species of the European lynx, which will be housed in another Rock Den section, yet to be completed.

The Siberian lynx, together with the Siberian tiger and Persian leopard, illustrates how a sub-species, living in the most northerly extent of that species' range, is usually much paler in colour than its counterparts living further south.

Cheetah

Unlike other cats, cheetahs cannot retract their claws into sheaths; as a result, the claws are not used as weapons, when hunting prey, but more as the spikes on an athlete's running shoes – gripping the ground as the cheetah catapults into short bursts of incredible speed. The lithe, slim body, long legs and small, light skull are all adaptations to running down, rather than ambushing, the small antelopes upon which it preys on the open plains.

Now extinct in India and exceedingly rare in Asia Minor, the cheetah is also severely threatened in Africa. Despite protection in many African national parks, its numbers continue to decline. One interesting theory for this is that, being daylight hunters, cheetahs are constantly harassed and followed by tourists in safari vehicles, thus putting the animals under great stress.

On the whole, cheetahs do not do well in captivity and only a few zoos are successful in breeding them, notably Whipsnade Zoo in this country. Research programmes are currently in operation, aiming to improve captive breeding worldwide, but it will be some time before the fastest land animal's future is assured in zoos.

For a number of years, Edinburgh Zoo has exhibited cheetahs in a very fine and spacious, naturalistic enclosure, but we have never bred them. Recently, we have divided the exhibit and built new dens, facilitating separation of the sexes when necessary, and, hopefully, increasing the chances of courtship behaviour.

MAP 57 LOCATION

Wolves

Closely resembling the animal from which all modern dogs are thought to be descended, today's wolf is the largest member of the dog family, which includes the foxes, coyotes, dingoes, Cape hunting dogs, bush dogs, jackals and others.

Found in a variety of habitats in the northern hemisphere, and, although exterminated throughout much of its range by man, the wolf is still fairly numerous. The animal is not the villain legend would have us believe, and no reliable records exist, either in Britain or America, of wolves actually killing humans.

Canadian Timber Wolf

The Zoo's timber wolves are exhibited in Wolf Wood, a stand of beech and sycamore trees near the summit of the Zoo hill. Although we have not bred our wolves for many years, our animals are fine specimens and, as one watches them through the trees, it is not difficult to imagine that, just over 200 years ago, they roamed wild in Scotland.

The Society has a larger breeding group of wolves at the Highland Wildlife Park near Kingussie. In the future, we will probably phase out wolves at Edinburgh Zoo and use their enclosure for either the rare maned wolf of South America or the African Cape hunting dog.

Bush Dog ▼

These odd-looking and non-typical members of the dog family are adapted to life in the tropical forests of Central and northern South America, where their short legs and long bodies assist them in rapid movement through dense undergrowth. They are also excellent swimmers. Bush dogs socialise in packs, and it is thought that these packs are made up of extended families. Hunting together, they prey on quite large forest rodents, such as pacas and agoutis, and even on small deer. They communicate by bird-like calls and screeches.

Our animals were donated to the Society in 1987 by Twycross Zoo and Kilverstone Wildlife Park, both zoos in which the species has bred. We hope very much to be successful with them, as up to six pups are born in a litter and the male participates in the rearing of the young – all the makings of a lively exhibit!

Coatimundi ▲

Coatimundis belong to the raccoon family and are found in the southern United States of America, Central America and a large part of South America. They are omnivores, eating mainly invertebrates and fruits.

Extremely active by day, they make a good exhibit as they forage with their flexible snouts and carry their tails aloft. They are very social creatures, groups of up to twenty five individuals being composed of several females and their young. In the wild, males join the groups only for mating but, in captivity, remain permanently with the others. They breed easily in zoos and the young are particularly playful and noisy as they chase each other up and down trees.

A male and two female ring-tailed coatis were acquired by the Zoo in 1987 and will be on view to the public early in 1988 in the newly-constructed continuation of the Rock Dens.

It is fashionable today to apply the name "coatimundi" to a single male only – females, or a group of the animals, are referred to as "coatis".

Otters

Otters belong to the family of carnivores which includes the weasels, stoats and pine martens. They hunt exclusively by or in water, feeding on fish, crustaceans and amphibians. There are several different species of otter and their ranges are widespread in Europe, Africa, Asia and North and South America. In many of their haunts, they have become very shy and difficult to observe, and indeed, very rare, due to disturbance of their habitat, pollution and persecution for their valuable fur.

Oriental Small-Clawed Otter

This is one of the smaller species of otter and is much more active by day than the larger European otter, formerly exhibited in the Zoo. Our otters arrived in 1987 and have given hours of pleasure to visitors as they play vigorously together and explore repeatedly every nook and cranny of their enclosure. One of them has taken to tree-climbing – the tree was there, so had to be explored!

Oriental small-clawed otters have particularly dexterous forepaws and manipulate food, pebbles and, in fact, anything they can "lay hands on"; our pair totally destroyed all the turfs and plants in the exhibit within a few days of taking up residence. An extension to the land area of the enclosure is planned which, together with the underfloor heating in the cubbing boxes, should provide ideal breeding conditions. Being one of the more social species of otter, and therefore more vocal, complete family groups can be excitingly displayed, even although the male does not take an active part in the rearing of the young.

Bears

There are seven species of bear, ranging in size from the giant Kodiak race of the brown bear to the diminutive Malayan sun bear of South East Asia. They are classed as the largest carnivores, but only the polar bear is almost exclusively so, feeding mainly on seals. Other bears, in addition to eating flesh, forage extensively for plants, fruit, bulbs, roots, wild honey, insects and other invertebrates. Bears walk on the soles of their feet and, despite their lumbering appearance, show a surprising turn of speed. Some species are agile tree-climbers.

Bears, especially polar bears, are considered by many zoo staff to be the most potentially dangerous animals in zoos, due to their unpredictable natures and to the fact that their relatively expressionless faces betray little of their current disposition.

European Brown Bear

All the brown bears of Europe, Asia and North America are accepted as being one species, merely different races. Some, such as the grizzly and Kodiak sub-species, are larger than others. Brown bears, like other bears, are solitary but will congregate together in mountain streams to fish for salmon, each laying claim to a territory in the river and scooping out the fish with their massive paws. They do not actually hibernate in winter but will spend long periods sleeping in dens or lairs.

Edinburgh Zoo has always exhibited brown bears and the Brown Bear Rock is one of our oldest enclosures. Yet it is modern in concept; the bears are at visitor eye-level and there are no visual barriers between the public and the animals. So often in the past bears were displayed in pits, hardly the most ideal of exhibits, either for the animals or the visitors. Cubs, often triplets, have been a regular sight on the Rock over the years. They are born in a secluded den usually in early January, and the female brings them out into the main enclosure about Easter. Brown bears are not endangered animals and it is sometimes difficult to place the cubs in other zoos.

In the near future, we hope to exhibit and breed the rare spectacled bear from South America which is less frequently seen in captivity.

Polar Bear

Ranging over incredible distances in the Arctic wastes, and often seen on pack ice many miles from land, the polar bear, in the wild, is most certainly a nomad. The record of captive breeding and rearing of cubs is not high in the world's zoos.

Our polar bear enclosure dates from 1913 and we realise it is far from ideal. We hope, in the future, to re-design and greatly extend it.

Our male bear was born and reared at Whipsnade Zoo in 1976 and our female was presented to the Society by the government of Manitoba in 1984. They are compatible animals and play well together, but so far we have not succeeded in breeding.

Pandas

Of the two members of this family, the giant panda from China is the more well-known, despite its great rarity and the fact that very few zoos are fortunate enough to acquire the species. Exhibited in captivity much more often, is the smaller red or lesser panda from the forests around the Himalayas.

The giant panda resembles a bear and the lesser panda, a raccoon. The opinion, now widely held, is that they are related both to bears and raccoons, but probably more so to bears. Despite being classed as carnivores, they eat mostly plant material which, in the wild, consists predominantly of bamboo.

Red or Lesser Panda

In March 1983, Edinburgh Zoo received its first pair of red or lesser pandas. Our two animals are totally unrelated so as to maximise our chances of successful breeding. We were advised on our choice of pandas (the male from Adelaide Zoo, Australia and the female from Marwell Zoo, England) by the International Studbook Keeper in Rotterdam, who holds the records of all the red pandas in the world's zoos.

After the male had undergone his quarantine period, the pair settled down very well in the former Raccoon Enclosure, where an additional three cubbing boxes had been erected to accommodate the female panda's habit, in the wild, of moving her young from nest to nest. Twins were born in the summer of 1985 – one died at birth, the other, sadly, at four months of age. In 1986, twins were again born and, although one died immediately, the other was mother-reared to adulthood and is now in Paignton Zoo with a mate of his own. In 1987 a single cub was born, successfully reared and is destined for Belfast Zoo, where he will be paired with a female from another zoo. Edinburgh Zoo was the only British organisation to breed red pandas in 1986 and 1987. The almost immediate death of one of the twins in 1985 and 1986 may indicate a dietary problem – so little is known of these animals in the wild – and zoos are working together to improve their husbandry of this species.

Our pandas spend much time climbing and sleeping high in their trees – look carefully for them, from all sides of the exhibit.

MAP
6
LOCATION

Seals and Sea Lions

Seals and sea lions, along with walruses, are a group of carnivorous mammals which spend the greater part of their lives at sea. They come ashore only to breed, to moult, sometimes to rest or sleep, and to bask in the warm sun. During the course of evolution, their feet and legs changed into flippers, hence their name – pinnipeds, meaning "fin-feet". Although agile in water, they are clumsy on land. Their bodies are streamlined, like those of fish, and they are insulated against the cold by a thick layer of blubber.

True seals have no external ears, whereas sea lions and fur seals have small, scroll-like external ear-flaps. Sea lions can bring their hind flippers forward, underneath their bodies, to assist them in movement on land, but true seals must heave themselves forward, using only their fore limbs, and drag their hindquarters behind them.

Grey or Atlantic Seal

Prior to 1980, our grey seals bred occasionally, but since 1981, the female has given birth to a pup each January. Now she is getting old and we do not expect such births to continue. The birth takes place on land, where the youngster remains for the first few weeks. Once weaned, the young seal is removed from the enclosure as the male tends to become aggressive.

Californian Sea Lion

Sea lions have bred and reared their pups in Edinburgh Zoo in the past but we have had no breeding since our current male took up residence in 1981. It is still possible that he may breed with our younger females.

The Sea Lion Pool dates from 1914 and provides plenty of space for the animals to dive and race for the fish, fed to them by the keepers at 3.00pm daily throughout the spring and summer. A live commentary accompanies this feeding session during the summer season.

MAP LOCATION 3

Rhinoceroses

Five species of rhinoceros exist today, looking very much as they did millions of years ago. Two species occur in Africa, each with two horns – the black rhino and the white or square-lipped rhino. Three come from Asia – the great Indian one-horned rhino, the Javan rhino (also with one horn) and the smallest and only hairy species – the Sumatran rhino, which has two horns. All are rare and highly endangered, three of them drastically so.

The downfall of the rhino is the belief, in the Far East, that its horn contains medicinal properties, capable of curing a wide range of complaints. Coupled with this, is the demand in recent years in North Yemen for ceremonial dagger handles fashioned from rhino horn. Particularly affected are the black rhinos of Africa, formerly the most numerous and wide-spread species, whose numbers in the last decade have plummeted alarmingly as poachers have taken a frightening toll.

The Indian rhino is well-protected in reserves in India and Nepal, and a few are bred in zoos, particularly Basle Zoo, but its present population, of just over 1700, is not high. There are no Javan rhinos in captivity at the time of going to press (February 1988) and their entire population is estimated at 50-70 animals in the Udjung Kulong Reserve in Java. The 200-300 surviving Sumatran rhinos, scattered in pockets throughout parts of South East Asia, are considered to have such a fragmented population that the World Wildlife Fund and the Indonesian government have initiated a captive breeding project, involving about eight recently-captured animals, as a safeguard against imminent extinction.

White or Square-Lipped Rhinoceros

Largest of the five species, the white rhinoceros is the only truly social one. After a near brush with extinction in the early 1900s, the southern sub-species has been managed so well in its native South Africa by the Game Department, that its present status within national parks, of over 4000 animals, is quite healthy but gives no cause for complacency. The northern sub-species in Uganda has been all but wiped out during the recent civil wars, when they received little protection.

Two white rhinos arrived here in 1976 from the large breeding herd at Whipsnade Zoo. Since then, the female has given birth successfully several times. It is thought we are only the fourth zoo in the world to breed from a pair rather than a group. The main breeding groups outside South Africa are at Whipsnade Zoo and San Diego Wild Animal Park.

Tapirs

Tapirs are shy, fairly nocturnal, forest-living animals, related to horses and rhinos by virtue of the fact that they have an "odd" (as opposed to "even") number of toes. Three species of tapir are found in the Americas and one in South East Asia. All are rare. Most dramatic in appearance is the black and white Malayan tapir, whilst the American species – the Brazilian tapir, the Mountain tapir and the Central American or Baird's tapir – are all brownish in colour. All tapirs give birth to brown infants, vividly patterned with cream stripes and spots.

Brazilian or South American Tapir

Probably the least rare of the four species, the Brazilian tapir shows the streamlined shape and rounded back of a dense forest-dweller. Adept at swimming, it can submerge with only its flexible trunk-like nose held above the water like a periscope.

Brazilian tapirs have been exhibited here for many years but we first successfully reared a baby only in 1984. Since then, we have had two further healthy offspring. The species does not breed readily in many zoos, and therefore we have no trouble in finding good homes for our youngsters.

Their future is uncertain, due to hunting and destruction of habitat, and so production of young in the world's zoos is essential.

MAP LOCATION 44

Zebras

Zebras belong to the same family as horses and asses – the equids – and occur only in Africa. The largest and, arguably, the most handsome species of zebra is the narrow-striped Grevy's zebra, which inhabits semi-arid regions of northern Kenya and southern Ethiopia, and is now becoming very rare. Also rare, are the mountain zebras of southern Africa. The most wide-ranging and numerous are the plains zebras, of which several sub-species are recognised, distinguishable by variations in the stripe pattern.

Grant's Zebra

Our Grant's zebras, a form of plains zebra from the East African grasslands, are exhibited in a small group, consisting of a stallion, several mares and their offspring.

Our zebras breed well – several foals usually being born each year. Surplus males are sent to other zoos and, in the recent past, we have supplied the zoos of Copenhagen, Belfast and Paignton with youngsters. The group on exhibit usually numbers seven or eight animals and, it is of interest that these zebras are completely acclimatised to Scottish weather on an exposed hillside; they require no heating in their stables, and the mares often give birth, quite successfully, in mid-winter. In the interests of maintaining genetic diversity, we have recently brought in a new stallion and retired our former breeding male, who had sired many foals over the years.

47

The Hippopotamus

There are two species of hippopotamus – the common hippo and the pygmy hippo. Both are found only in Africa. Having four toes on each foot, their closest relatives are pigs, but hippos are strictly vegetarian. Both kinds of hippo have huge canine and incisor teeth which have no function in their feeding habits, but are used to great effect in aggression and self-defence. Grass is cropped with the lips.

The common hippo is by far the larger of the two species and is also the more aquatic, spending most of the daylight hours practically submerged in rivers and lakes and coming ashore at night to feed.

Pygmy Hippo

The pygmy hippo is much rarer than the better-known common hippo, and its range is restricted to one or two places in West Africa. A true forest-dweller, it lives a fairly solitary existence, unlike that of its gregarious cousin.

Edinburgh Zoo has kept pygmy hippos for years but did not succeed until 1981 in breeding this species. Our eventual success was no doubt due to the exchange of individuals through inter-zoo co-operation, and young have been born regularly since then. In 1987 Edinburgh Zoo produced the first <u>male</u> pygmy hippo calf to be born in a British Zoo for a number of years. As a result, he was a very precious youngster, and although "booked" by Whipsnade Zoo,

may well spend part of his adult life "touring"! When our female has young, the male hippo is housed and exhibited separately, as the adults can be very aggressive towards each other. In fact some zoos put males and females together only for mating.

Now very rare in West Africa, little is known of the animals' habits in the wild. Fortunately, a number of zoos breed them regularly, Basle Zoo having a particularly good record. We are keen to pursue our success with this species as its future may well depend upon a bank of healthy, captive-bred stock from the breeding programmes of the world's zoos.

Deer

The characteristic feature of deer is that the males have bony antlers which are shed and regrown each year. Exceptions to this rule are the musk deer and the Chinese water deer, two species of which neither sex possesses antlers, and the reindeer, the only species of which both males and females have antlers. There are 31 species of deer, inhabiting Europe, Asia and the Americas and ranging in size from the moose to the tiny pudu.

Père David's Deer

First brought to the attention of the western world in 1865 by the French missionary/naturalist, Père Armand David, these Chinese deer, which now bear his name, became extinct in their homeland before the turn of the century. Fortunately, the missionary had been instrumental in having some sent to zoos in Europe and, from these few specimens, the current world population of well over 1000 animals has been bred. This was due to the efforts of the Dukes of Bedford who initiated the breeding programme at Woburn and then sent groups of the animals to zoos all over the world. This captive-breeding success story came full cycle when, in 1986, thirty nine deer from British zoos were re-introduced to China and released into a specially created wildlife reserve north of Shanghai.

MAP LOCATION 64

The Zoo's breeding group of muntjac occupies a hilly, wooded enclosure, providing them with ample cover in the summer season.

Red Deer

Red deer exist in Europe, Asia and North America. In North America they are known as wapiti or elk and are larger than their counterparts in Europe and Asia. They are Scotland's largest land mammal and, during the autumn breeding season or "rut", the bellowing of the stags, as they round up their females, can be heard reverberating through the Scottish hillsides.

A stag and several hinds are exhibited in the Zoo and calves are born each June.

Southern Pudu ▲

Smallest of all the deer, South American pudus are becoming increasingly rare.

In Edinburgh Zoo the pudus are housed in paddocks adjoining those of the little Maxwell's duiker antelopes. Visitors may be interested to compare the two species, which have evolved in different parts of the world to occupy similar habitats and lead similar lifestyles.

The Zoo has had considerable success in breeding this animal which, like the duiker antelope, is best kept in pairs.

Reeves Muntjac ▶

Muntjac, from South East Asia, are also known as barking deer, because, when excited or alarmed, they give a very loud, short, sharp call. Males have long upper-canine teeth, used as weapons.

Antelopes

Many people confuse antelopes and deer, but in one respect they are very different from each other. Unlike the antlers of a deer, which are shed and regrown annually, the horns of an antelope grow to their full extent and then remain unaltered throughout the animal's life. These horns have a bony core and an outer sheath of keratin and, although their shape may vary greatly from species to species, they never branch into tines as antlers do. In many antelope species, females, as well as males, carry horns.

85 species of antelope are recognised and they are found in a variety of habitats, mainly in Africa, but also in Asia. They range in size from the eland (as big as an ox) to the tiny royal antelope (hardly larger than a hare). Most antelopes of the plains, deserts and open areas are herd animals, whereas those of the forests are solitary or live in pairs.

Lechwe Antelope

Edinburgh Zoo has an excellent record in breeding the lechwe antelope. Our original females came from Zambia and the males from Chester Zoo, where there is also a breeding herd. These animals are adapted to live in marshy conditions in the wild, hence the provision of a large pool in their enclosure. The breeding group consists of a mature male, several females and their young. Two or three young are born in our herd annually and, in order to introduce a new bloodline into our stock, we imported a breeding male from Czechoslovakia, early in 1987. His first offspring were born at the turn of the year.

All the male youngsters, at eighteen months of age, are removed from the breeding herd and join a bachelor herd in the African Plains Exhibit, where they constitute a valuable "bank" of surplus males, on hand, should they be required by this or another zoo. Due to the absence of female lechwes, no serious aggression occurs within the group. Only male lechwe carry horns and, seen together, these six or seven males are an impressive sight, adding considerably to the visual impact of the mixed exhibit.

(MAP LOCATION 8) (MAP LOCATION 74)

Scimitar-Horned Oryx

The scimitar-horned oryx is one of three species of oryx antelope, all of which inhabit dry regions. Both sexes of the species carry formidable horns, which, on occasion, are used to fend off predators, sometimes injuring them fatally. Oryx horns have another claim to fame – the origin of the unicorn legend is probably the white Arabian oryx which, when seen in profile, can appear one-horned.

The scimitar-horned oryx, from the edge of the Sahara, is becoming increasingly rare, due to hunting and overgrazing of its habitat by domestic stock. Operation Scimitar Oryx is a consortium of organisations, including the Royal Zoological Society of Scotland, formed to co-ordinate

research on oryx, both in the wild and in captivity, with the aim of securing their survival in national reserves.

Our herd has made a significant contribution to this breeding programme and the first of our many oryx births took place in August 1983. Together with others from Whipsnade and Marwell zoos, three of our oryx calves were reintroduced to Tunisia, in the Bou-Hedma National Park, in December 1985. One of our animals gave birth to a calf in 1987. The last wild oryx seen in Tunisia was in 1906.

Addax Antelope

As is the case with the scimitar-horned oryx, the population of the addax, a desert antelope from northern Africa, is declining and captive-born specimens are required to restock certain areas in the wild such as the Bou-Hedma National Park.

We received our pair in 1985 from Marwell Zoo and since then, three male calves have been born. We expect to have further success with this handsome and unusual species.

colour from the female – an aid to recognition known as sexual dimorphism.

Within our blackbuck herd, we have exchanged individuals with other zoos, in an attempt to achieve a better balance of unrelated animals and so ensure more successful breeding.

Maxwell's Duiker

For many years, Edinburgh Zoo has maintained a number of breeding pairs of Maxwell's duiker – a shy, forest-living antelope from West Africa, seldom seen in zoos. This is one of the smaller species of duiker, whose Afrikaans name means "diver" – the animal literally dives for cover, when alarmed. Maxwell's duikers are best kept in adult male/female pairs, which is the probable group structure in the wild. Improving our breeding strain with this species is difficult, due to its scarcity in other zoos.

Blackbuck

These herd antelopes from the plains of India are our only Asian species. Now, greatly reduced in number in the wild state, the blackbuck was the original "antelope" – the name being used initially for this animal alone.

Like the lechwe, only the male blackbuck carries horns, but, unlike the lechwe, the male blackbuck differs in

SERVICES

TIMES OF OPENING

Edinburgh Zoo is open every day of the year, including Christmas Day and New Year's Day.
Summer **9.00**am until **6.00**pm
Winter **9.00**am until **5.00**pm (or dusk)
Sundays open at **9.30**am all year round.

CAR AND COACH PARK

The Car and Coach Park is situated behind the Post House Hotel, next to the Zoo Entrance. There is no charge for coaches bringing organised parties, and their drivers have free admission to the Park. Entry to the Park is through the Main Entrance only. A one-way turnstile below the Bird House **exits** into the Car Park.

PUSHCHAIRS AND WHEELCHAIRS

Children's pushchairs can be hired from the Main Entrance and a number of wheelchairs are available free of charge.

TOILET FACILITIES

Toilets are marked on the Zoo Map. Those allowing access for wheelchairs are in the Penguins' Pantry and adjoining the Car Park. The Penguins' Pantry Ladies' Toilet has a room for nursing mothers.

REFRESHMENTS

Hot meals and snacks are on sale in the Penguins' Pantry, which is also licensed. In the summer, The Den is also open, selling cold snacks and drinks. Kiosks, situated round the Zoo, sell ice cream, soft drinks and confectionery.

PICNICS

Picnics can be enjoyed on the many grassy areas in the Zoo or at the picnic tables beside The Steading. In wet weather picnics may be eaten in The Den.

LOST CHILDREN AND LOST PROPERTY

Staff are instructed to take all lost children to the Main Entrance. Please report any article lost or found to the Main Entrance.

FIRST AID

First aid is available at the Main Entrance and the Members' House.

PUBLIC TELEPHONES

There is a public telephone beside the Penguins' Pantry and also one outside the Main Entrance.

ZOO SHOPS

A well-stocked Bookshop, specialising in natural history books for all ages, adjoins the Education Centre. The Zoo Shop is opposite and sells a wide range of souvenirs. A new shop is planned at the Main Entrance for 1989.

FILM AND PHOTOGRAPHY

Colour films are on sale in the Zoo Shop and also in the Kiosks. Visitors are free to photograph any of the exhibits with still or movie cameras. Cameras may be borrowed from the Zoo Shop for a returnable deposit of £20.

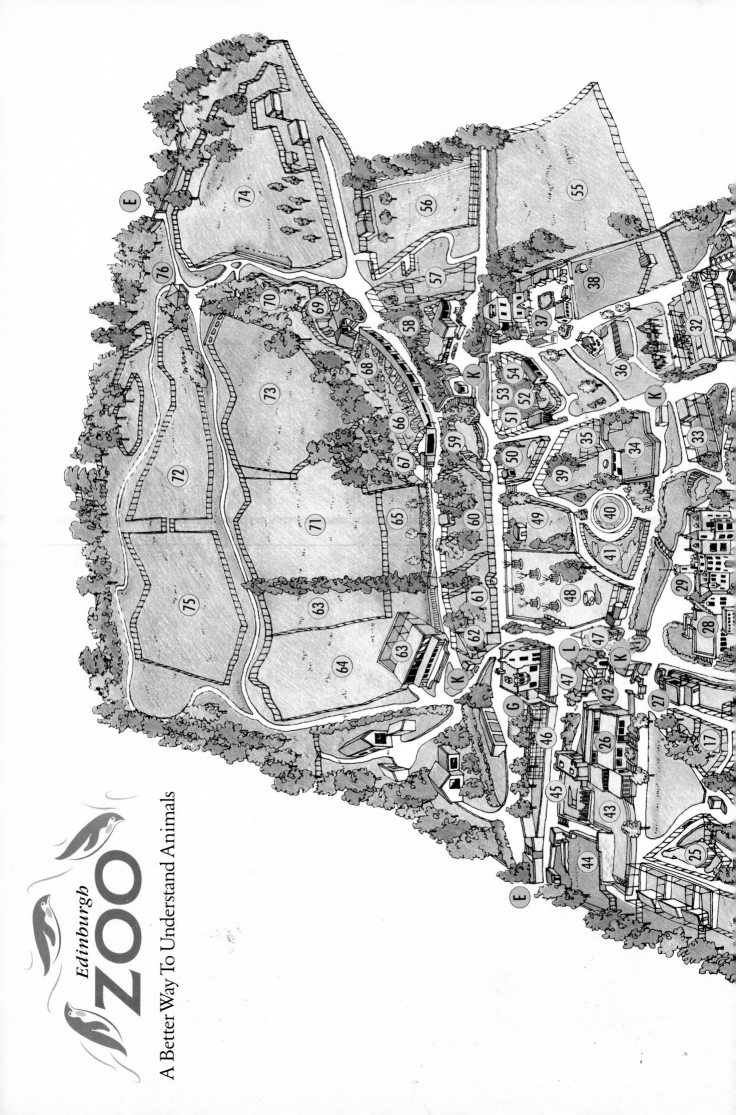

CAR PARK

CORSTORPHINE ROAD

1 Waldrapp Ibis Aviary
2 Duck Ponds
3 Sea Lion
4 Rhea
5 White Stork
6 Red Panda
7 Otter Pool
8 Lechwe Antelope
9 Pheasant Aviaries
10 Capybara
11 Pelican and Black Swan
12 Penguin Nursery
13 Polar Bear
14 Kangaroo
15 Parma Wallaby
16 The Den
17 Proposed Penguin Exhibit
   Extension
18 Barbary Sheep/Collared Peccary
19 Grey Seal
20 Monkey House
21 Duiker Antelope/Pudu Deer
22 Stump-Tailed Macaque
23 Gorilla
24 Addax Antelope
25 Gentoo and King Penguin
26 Education Centre
27 Zoo Shop
28 Penguins' Pantry
29 Members' House
30 Reptile House and Bird House
31 Parrot Garden
32 Chimpanzee
33 Siamang
34 Pygmy Hippo
35 Wattled Crane
36 Marmoset Complex
37 Brass Rubbing Centre
38 The Steading and Picnic Area
39 Cassowary
40 Prairie Dog
41 Beaver
42 Bookshop
43 Giraffe
44 Tapir

45 Elephant
46 Elephant Walk Aviaries
47 Birds of Prey Aviaries
48 Rhino
49 Capybara
50 Flamingo
51 Wildcat/Jungle Cat
52 Brown Bear
53 Owl Aviaries
54 Small Carnivores
55 Farm Field
56 Blackbuck
57 Cheetah
58 Lion Rock
59 Barbary Macaque
60 Muntjac Deer
61 Vietnamese Pig
62 Golden Eagle
63 Camel
64 Père David's Deer
65 Kangaroo and Wallaby
66 Coatimundi
67 Rockhopper Penguin
68 Lynx, Leopards, Jaguar
69 Tiger
70 Wolf
71 Red Deer
72 Soay Sheep
73 Highland Cattle
74 African Plains – Zebra/Oryx/
   Lechwe
75 Guanaco
76 Hilltop Viewpoint

K Confectionery Kiosks
G Gentlemen's Toilet
L Ladies' Toilet
0 Main Office
E Exits
0C Orientation Centre and
   Entrance Development

The location of animals may
be subject to change.

EVENTS AND ACTIVITIES

ORIENTATION CENTRE

The Zoo's Orientation Centre, at the proposed new Main Entrance, will be opened on 30 June 1988 by Her Majesty the Queen, and will be a must for all visitors to the Park. Its purpose is to offer advice on how best to use your time in the Zoo and to illustrate the Zoo's role today.

ANIMAL CONTACT SESSIONS

During Easter and summer school holidays, and at weekends in May and June, 50-minute animal contact sessions are held in the Education Centre for children and adults to look more closely at and touch some of the smaller animals. When possible, these are held six times daily.

PENGUIN PARADE

From April to September, every day at **2.30**pm, the king and gentoo penguins parade across the grassy area in front of their enclosure. In March and October, **weather permitting** they parade at **2.15**pm.

FEEDING TIMES
Sea Lions
  1 April – 30 September **3.00**pm
  1 October – 31 March **2.30**pm
Penguins
  1 April – 30 September **2.45**pm
  1 October – 31 March **2.15**pm
Grey Seals
  following penguins
Big Cats
  for health reasons, the big cats are fed on a varying routine so exact times cannot be guaranteed.

Please do not feed our animals. All are on specially prepared diets and extra or unsuitable food can harm them.

Please help us to keep the Zoo tidy by using the litter bins provided.

BRASS RUBBING

Make your own Brass Rubbings of endangered animals at the Brass Rubbing Centre in The Steading, open **12.30 – 4.30**pm, from 1 April – 31 August. Paper and wax are provided at a reasonable cost.

INFORMATION STATIONS

During peak seasons a number of Information Stations are manned in selected parts of the Zoo, offering activities, "hands-on" items and leaflets relating to certain animals.

Please check Notice Board in Orientation Centre or, prior to opening of Orientation Centre, the "WHAT'S ON?" leaflet handed out at Paydesk for details and times of these activities.

Please keep children safe and do not allow them to cross safety barriers or stray onto flower beds.

No pets are allowed into the Zoo, including dogs.

African Plains Exhibit

This extensive and undulating paddock, broken by trees and grassy knolls, is practically on the summit of the Zoo hill and offers spectacular views of the city and its surroundings. It is ideal as a mixed exhibit for herd species. Here, with unimpeded views of the animals, due to a hidden ha-ha ditch separating them from the visitor, one can watch the interaction amongst breeding groups of Grant's zebras and scimitar-horned oryx antelopes, and a bachelor herd of lechwe antelopes. Although their ranges would not overlap in the wild, the three species coexist well. The oryx appear to be dominant over the zebra and the lechwe. The exhibit itself has posed no major management problems.

MAP LOCATION 74

Cattle and Sheep

Various species of wild cattle and wild sheep inhabit different parts of the world today. It is commonly believed that all breeds of domestic cattle in the western world are descended from a large, ox-like forest dweller, called the auroch – now extinct. Domestic sheep probably originated from an animal resembling the mouflon, still found wild in Sardinia.

Domestic Breeds

Near the Zoo's summit is a breeding herd of the shaggy and hardy Highland cattle, well-adapted to Scotland's wind, rain and sleet and able to survive on poor grazing.

We also have a flock of Soay sheep, thought to resemble the first domesticated sheep brought to Britain around 3000BC. Isolated on off-shore islands, like Soay, they have retained their original characteristics, such as small size and light wool, and have not been affected by interbreeding.

Near the Steading is a small group of St. Kilda or four-horned sheep – another primitive breed from the Hebrides.

Barbary Sheep

Sure-footed climbers of the mountains of northern Africa, Barbary sheep are sometimes referred to as "goat-sheep".

Although classed as true sheep, they have several goat-like characteristics.

Most of the water they require is obtained from mountain plants. Rival males clash their horns together or, sometimes, link horns and grapple, trying to pull each other down.

Although common in zoos and easy to breed in captivity, Barbary sheep are becoming rarer in the wild, due to hunting. Lambs are born every year in Edinburgh Zoo.

Pigs and Peccaries

Pigs and hogs are even-toed, hoofed mammals, with long snouts, and they are found in all continents except Australia. Wild pigs include the wild boar, bush pig, giant forest hog and warthog, many of which have long, fearsome tusks. It is thought that the wild boar of Europe and Asia is probably the ancestor of all domestic pigs. Peccaries are pig-like mammals from America which differ in several ways from true pigs, for example, in the arrangement of their teeth, the formation of the stomach and toes, and by having a scent gland situated on the back. All pigs and peccaries are social animals.

programme within British zoos is well-managed: we are not allowed to import any members of the pig family into Britain, as a legal protection against the possible introduction of swine fever to our country's livestock.

Collared Peccary

Collared peccaries come from America and our breeding group arrived in the Zoo in March 1986. At the end of the year the first birth occurred – a male. We were delighted by this quick success and in 1987 twins were born to another female. Although collared peccaries are not particularly rare in the wild, it is essential that a breeding

Vietnamese Pot-Bellied Pig

Edinburgh Zoo has for several years kept a group of these domestic pigs which originate from South East Asia. This is one of the smallest breeds of domestic pig and, like all of its kind, will eat, in addition to roots and plants, a certain amount of animal matter. These Vietnamese pigs are kept in a wooded area which suits them very well, as they can root amongst the trees.

61

Camels and Guanacos

Two species of camel exist today – the one-humped Arabian camel or dromedary and the two-humped Bactrian camel. There are no wild Arabian camels – all are domesticated and have served man for centuries as "ships of the desert". The much heavier-built Bactrian camel is also domesticated and used as a beast of burden in Central Asia, but a number of them are still truly wild in the Gobi Desert.

Related to camels are the guanacos, vicunas, llamas and alpacas of South America. Llamas and alpacas exist only as domesticated animals; guanacos and vicunas are wild animals.

Arabian Camel

Edinburgh Zoo used to exhibit both varieties of camel but now maintains a breeding group of only the Arabian species.

Despite their various adaptations to desert conditions, camels have acclimatised well to Scottish weather and can be seen out in their paddocks even in snow.

MAP LOCATION 63

Guanaco

We also exhibit and regularly breed the guanaco, the wild ancestor of the llama. These hardy animals thrive on their exposed enclosure at the summit of the Zoo hill. Guanacos breed well in zoos but are becoming rarer in the wild. Vicunas, formerly threatened in the wild because of the demand for their wool – which is considered to be the finest in the world – are now increasing in number.

MAP LOCATION 75

Giraffes

Like cattle, sheep, antelopes and deer, giraffes are plant-eating ruminants, i.e. they chew the cud. They live in loosely-connected herds amongst the acacia woodlands on the savannahs. Like their relatives, the okapis, they are found only in Africa. There are several races of giraffe, differing slightly in their markings, and all can interbreed, as indeed they do where their ranges meet.

Giraffes are considered to be "successful" animals; although their range in Africa is somewhat reduced, they are not an endangered species. Due to their great height (males can grow to 18 feet) they do not compete with other animals for their food source – the leaves of trees. The height factor, coupled with their excellent vision, ensures that giraffes are seldom caught by lions, their only enemy apart from man. Giraffes are not, on the whole, harassed by man; they do little harm to crops, and apart from walking through the occasional fence, they do nothing to incur man's wrath or irritation. The only use that man has made of the giraffe is to fashion the tail hairs into flywhisks and bracelets.

Baringo or Rothschild's Giraffe

Our present group of giraffes is of the Baringo or Rothschild's variety, distinguished by their pale lower legs and "blotchy" markings, often with a darker centre. They are found in western Kenya and Uganda.

Although giraffes have been exhibited in Edinburgh Zoo through-out the years, we had no success in breeding them. This was surprising as they breed quite well in captivity as a rule.

In September 1983 a pair of young captive-bred giraffes was received by the Zoo, the last of our former group of giraffes having died. The Giraffe Enclosure was greatly extended and upgraded, and, as the animals settled down well, we had high hopes of at last celebrating a giraffe birth at Edinburgh. On 28 February 1987 we were re-warded by the arrival of a 5'10" healthy male baby giraffe. As his parents were only five years old at the time of his birth, we look forward to a new era at Edinburgh Zoo as far as giraffe breeding is concerned.

Male giraffe calves do not usually remain in the Zoo of their birth, as rivalry would eventually ensue between them and the breeding males. If they are to be transported to another zoo by road, this must be done before they are too tall to travel under motor-way bridges!

Rodents

The most successful and widespread family of mammals is that of the rodents, accounting for about half of all mammal species – nearly 2000 in number. They range in size from the capybara to the pygmy mouse and include, amongst others, rats, porcupines, beavers, hamsters and squirrels. All are gnawing animals and their chisel-like incisor teeth grow continuously. Having short gestation periods and often large litter sizes, they are very numerous. Many burrow, some swim and others climb trees.

Canadian Beaver

Renowned for their industriousness and for their ability to fell trees, beavers demonstrate the rodents' gnawing skills to perfection. Using tree branches, mud and stones, they build dams and construct "lodges" in ponds, with underwater entrances.

Acouchi

One of many species of small, long-legged rodents from the South American forests, acouchis have a lifestyle similar to that of forest antelopes in Africa. The Zoo's breeding acouchis are exhibited with common marmosets, a combination which might well occur in the wild. Our animals originally came to us as a confiscation, by HM Customs, of an illegal consignment of animals, destined for a dealer.

We have bred beavers on several occasions, our success doubtless due to the fact that our beavers are allowed to lead almost natural lives: they have excavated their own underground chambers, similar to lodges, which they enter, as in the wild, from under the water. In addition, we support dead trees in metal sockets in their exhibit, so that they may gnaw them down.

Capybara

The largest rodent is the capybara from South America which lives near ponds, lakes and rivers. They live in family units and, with their webbed toes, are good swimmers.

Edinburgh Zoo has an excellent record in the breeding of capybaras, with numerous incidences of twins and triplets being reared and recently, litters of quads and sextuplets, all surviving to adulthood. We now have two breeding pairs of capybaras in the

Zoo. Due to exchange of individuals with other zoos, none of our breeding animals are related.

Prairie Dog

Known as "dogs" because of the sharp warning bark they give, on sighting predators, prairie dogs live in extensive underground networks, called "towns", on the North American prairies.

Like the Zoo's beavers, our prairie dogs have complete freedom with regard to their lives below ground – there is no interference from Zoo staff in the "town" they have created under the mound of their enclosure, and they can often be seen ensuring that the rims, on the entrances to their burrows, are in good order. Since the recent acquisition of new animals, we now have a thriving and lively colony, six young having been born in 1987.

Marsupials

Apart from the oppossums of the Americas, all the other 200 or so marsupial species are confined to Australasia, where they have evolved, in virtual isolation, for millions of years. The unique characteristic of marsupials is that the young are born very tiny and under-developed: development continues in the pouch, where the milk teats are situated.

Parma Wallaby

Man's effect on the wildlife of Australia, through the introduction of alien species, has resulted in the decline in population of many of the smaller marsupials. Parma wallabies were thought to be extinct until a group was rediscovered on the island of Kawau, off New Zealand, where they had been introduced in 1870. (MAP LOCATION 15)

Bennett's Wallaby

Often seen in zoos, these wallabies breed readily in captivity and are well acclimatized to our climate – a group of them have now established themselves in Derbyshire, having escaped from a private zoo in 1940! (MAP LOCATION 65)

Western Grey Kangaroo ▼

Edinburgh Zoo has two breeding groups of the grey kangaroo. Young can often be seen in the pouches of our females. They illustrate well the large hindlegs and strong, balancing tail of the bounding marsupials. (MAP LOCATION 14) (MAP LOCATION 65)

Elephants

There are two species of elephant – the Asiatic and the African. Today, their future is severely threatened. African elephants have long been the target of poachers, trading in ivory, and their sharply declining numbers, in most African countries, are giving real cause for concern. To these intensely social animals, which often roam vast areas in their quest for food, less and less of their natural habitat is available, as man encroaches on their ranges in both continents.

Few of either species have been bred in zoos, because most organisations cannot afford to build the kind of accommodation, necessary to house male elephants.

African Elephant

Edinburgh Zoo's female African elephant, aged 21 years in 1988, and resident in the Park for 12 years, has now become an anomaly within our collection and her presence here runs contrary to all that the Zoo stands for. She is now our only example of a single specimen, not in a viable breeding group.

We are considering her possible transfer to some other zoo, which could offer company or, ideally, opportunity for breeding, but, even if a move were possible, it may not be to her advantage. She may not integrate with strange animals. She has strong bonds with her keepers, who spend considerable time with her, looking after her well, and she is a good-natured and tractable creature. At present, she

is being trained to accept a chain round her foot so that, when necessary, she can readily be examined by the Zoo vet. If she leaves Edinburgh, we have to be very sure that it is in her best interests.

MAP 45 LOCATION

69

Penguins

There are 18 species of penguin, all found in the southern hemisphere, but by no means all confined to the Antarctic. None can fly, but all swim well: their ancestors, 100 million years ago, gave up flight in favour of underwater hunting. At speeds of more than 25mph they "fly" under the water, using their stiff, blade-like wings, steering with their feet and tails, and leaping out of the water, like dolphins, to breathe.

The largest species is the emperor penguin, nesting in the frozen Antarctic wastes, and the smallest is the fairy penguin from the southern coasts of Australia, nesting amongst the roots of beach plants or in burrows.

The bodies of all penguins are covered with short feathers, not fur, as may appear at first glance. In addition to the feathers, pads of fat, underneath the skin, help to keep the birds warm in cold extremes. All penguins have dark backs and white fronts, possibly camouflaging them from the fish they hunt and also from their main enemy, the leopard seal.

Edinburgh Zoo is world-famous for its penguins. It is universally recognised as the foremost zoo in the breeding of gentoo penguins and in the number exhibited. Two of our penguin colonies were originally established with the assistance of the Salvesen Whaling Company, which provided a regular supply of penguins from the Antarctic, in our earlier years. As time passed, much was learned at Edinburgh about the care of penguins, and which species thrived best in our climate. Eventually the Zoo concentrated on two species – the king and the gentoo. Since 1963, with the ending of Britain's whaling activities, no wild gentoo or king penguins have been brought into Edinburgh Zoo. Since that year our colonies have been self-perpetuating. In the 1940s, Edinburgh Zoo established a small colony of rockhopper penguins.

Gentoo Penguin

These birds are found in large colonies on barren islands near the Antarctic, and it is with this species that Edinburgh Zoo has its greatest success.

The number of gentoos in the Zoo is kept at approximately 80 individuals. In mid-March, the stone nesting rings, filled with pebbles, are arranged in the enclosure according to the same pattern as that of previous years. The birds are always awaiting the arrival of the rings, already paired – in 86% of cases, with the same partner as before.

There is great activity at this time, as males court the females by offering pebbles, and both sexes give vent to penetrating calls. Usually two eggs are laid, but not always both chicks are hatched. The eggs hatch in May and the young are fed by their parents on regurgitated fish, for two months, after which they are taught to accept whole fish from the keeper's hand.

Between 20 and 30 young are safely reared each year: some of them are sent to zoos as far away as Japan, but others are reintroduced to our own colony.

Rockhopper Penguin

These little penguins inhabit islands around Tristan da Cunha and are so-named because of their habit of hopping, with both feet together, from ledge to ledge on quite high rocky coastlines. They have strong claws with which they grip the rocks.

Until several years ago, we had little success with this species, chicks always dying at about three weeks of age. Now, with some eggs being artificially incubated, and youngsters either being hand-reared or at least given periods of hand-feeding, we are now building a sizeable colony of rockhoppers.

MAP LOCATION 67

King Penguin

Perhaps the public's favourite, the king penguin is the second largest species and is a true Antarctic dweller. These birds lay a single egg, which is balanced on the feet and protected by a flap of skin. Initially the chicks stand between the adult's feet for protection and are kept warm by the brood skin. For ten months the young are covered in brown down and cannot swim until the adult plumage grows in.

This is a much smaller colony than that of the gentoos, numbering 20 – 25 birds. Some eggs are taken for artificial incubation and some are left with the birds. Hatchings balance deaths and our colony remains stable.

MAP LOCATION 25

The sex of a penguin is not obvious to humans, and has to be determined by observation of breeding pairs. All our penguins are fitted with a metal flipper band, bearing a number. This identifies the penguin and allows us to ascribe to it its age and sex. The numbers in our penguin colonies afford excellent opportunities for research, undertaken by the staff and university students.

Our penguins are hand-fed on whole, ungutted fish plus supplementary vitamins.

An event not to be missed, is the daily "parade" of penguins around the area in front of their enclosure, usually two-thirds of the king and gentoo colonies joining in.

The king and gentoo penguins are exhibited together in the centre of the Zoo and their enclosure is due to be redesigned in the near future, incorporating viewing of the birds underwater. The nursery is adjacent to the polar bears, but a new nursery is part of the planned extended exhibit. The rockhopper exhibit has recently been upgraded and is further up the Zoo hill.

Large Flightless Birds

The ostrich, emu, rhea and cassowary are all large, flightless birds. They are descended from flying birds, but have developed their great size at the expense of their power of flight. All of them are excellent runners, with strong, powerful legs and feet.

Australian Cassowary

Cassowaries are solitary birds of the forests of northern Australia and Papua New Guinea, the sexes only coming together to mate. The bony helmet, or casque, prevents the head being injured by low-hanging branches as they run.

Incubation of the eggs is the responsibility solely of the male, as is the rearing of the chicks. The striped chicks go through a golden-brown colour phase before developing the blue-black adult plumage at about four years of age.

Having hatched the first cassowary chicks in Britain in 1967, Edinburgh Zoo is still one of the very few zoos which breed this bird. Since then, we have bred them consistently, from a variety of adults. In order to simulate the conditions in the wild, the female must be separated from the male, once she has laid her complete clutch of eggs. The male has then to be encouraged to sit on these eggs, on a nest of peat, in one of the Cassowary Sheds. Naturally, our cassowary chicks are much sought ▶ after, by other zoos.

Common Rhea

Unlike the cassowary, the South American rhea inhabits open country and avoids forests. They are social birds, one cock and several hens being the normal group size, but after the breeding season, they often flock together in larger numbers.

The male rhea incubates the eggs of a number of females and rears the chicks. The male at Edinburgh Zoo has not, as yet, fulfilled this role, but, hopefully, it will only be a matter of time before we have a large flock, as, usually, they breed readily in captivity.

Birds of Prey

Included in this group of birds, known as the raptors, are the hawks and eagles, the falcons and the owls, all of which are splendidly equipped in one way or another to locate, catch and kill their various forms of prey. Superb eyesight, incredible turns of speed in swooping and diving, powerful talons for gripping and piercing, and sharp, hooked beaks for tearing are some of the features exhibited by such birds. Birds of prey are found in most temperate and tropical regions of the world, and certain species inhabit even the polar areas. The largest British bird of prey is the golden eagle.

Owls

As we are specialising in various owls, the group of aviaries below the Lion Rock is now given over entirely to these birds. The soft feathers of an owl allow it to fly silently, thus giving the prey no warning. The acute hearing of the owl enables it, in the silence, to hear the slightest sound made by the prey. Most owls are perfectly camouflaged against their typical backgrounds.

Snowy Owl

The Zoo's greatest success, regarding birds of prey, is undoubtedly with the snowy owl, the silent hunter of the far north. This owl is unusual in that it hunts by day and is not nocturnal, like most other owls. Edinburgh Zoo's first snowy owl chick was hatched in 1971. Since then we have progressed to an average annual rearing of six chicks. Our snowy owls have now bred to the second generation. They are in great demand by other zoos, but it is our policy to advise all prospective buyers, who desire a pair, to purchase one sex from Edinburgh and the other from some other zoo. Such action ensures a healthier strain of captive bird. Our

snowy owl chicks can be seen with their parents during May/June and all together in a separate enclosure in July/August.

European eagle owls are bred regularly in the Zoo (photo left), and, in recent years, we have acquired pairs of Savigny's eagle owl, MacKinder's eagle owl, the Abyssinian eagle owl, the great-horned owl and, also, Boobook's owl. Although we have as yet had no success in breeding the latter five species, we hope that, in time, these birds will follow the example set by our snowy owls and European eagle owls.

MAP
53
LOCATION

77

Golden Eagle

Severely threatened, the golden eagle inhabits wild, mountainous country in the Highlands, the Hebrides and other parts of Scotland, and of Ireland. It continues to breed despite setbacks brought about by man's use of chemical sprays to protect crops. The poison in the sprays is absorbed by the eagles' prey and, in turn, contaminates the eagle, with the possible result of affecting its breeding. This was the case with the poisonous chemicals formerly used in sheep dip, which the eagles ingested through scavenging on the carcases of sheep on the hills.

Golden eagles have been exhibited in Edinburgh Zoo for many years and although eggs have been laid, they have always been infertile. Early in 1982 it was discovered whilst the birds were being sexed, using a surgical technique, that the male of our pair was sexually inactive.

Fortunately, we were able to replace him with a different bird which sadly died soon afterwards. Since then, we have attempted to artificially inseminate our female eagle but with no success so far. Very recently we have been lucky to acquire an injured male eagle. The two birds have adjusted well to each other and hopes are high that a natural mating will occur. The female has already proved herself in incubating eggs, and rearing an introduced buzzard chick.

MAP LOCATION 62

Buzzard

We also exhibit and breed buzzards – sometimes mistaken for golden eagles, but only by persons who have never seen a golden eagle. The buzzards are actually considerably smaller.

MAP LOCATION 47

All birds of prey, their nests and eggs are well protected by law in Great Britain. Under the Wildlife and Countryside Act any captive falcon must be registered with the Department of the Environment and a licence obtained for it. Any endangered species of falcon received at Edinburgh Zoo is sent to one of the various hawk trusts, which specialise in captive breeding.

All birds of prey exhibited here, other than those which are Zoo bred, have been handed in to us, injured and in need of care.

Pheasants and Peafowl

Both peafowl and pheasants, being ground nesters, are good examples of species in which the female is drab and camouflaged, thus protecting her eggs and chicks, while the male is brilliantly plumed in the breeding season, in order to attract the females. However, this is not true of all the forty nine species of pheasant – in several of the species, the sexes look the same or similar. Edinburgh Zoo exhibits and breeds the common peafowl and a number of pheasant species.

The Pheasants

The Zoo's breeding pheasants are housed in a group of aviaries which radiate from a central block containing the shelter areas. Pheasants, surplus to the breeding stock, are exhibited with the common peafowl in the Wallaby Paddocks. Quite a number of species feature in the Zoo's breeding programme, including, amongst others, the golden pheasant (left), the Lady Amherst's pheasant (above), the Monal pheasant and Reeves pheasant. Conservation projects are being undertaken, an example of which is the re-introduction of the cheer pheasant to its former range in Pakistan, where it became extinct in the 1970s. Edinburgh Zoo's cheer pheasants help to publicise the plight of this bird and its relatives.

In the aviaries behind the Elephant Enclosure are exhibited grey peacock pheasants and Siamese fireback pheasants. At present, the rare Edward's pheasant is in our collection along with the three species of eared pheasant – the blue, the brown and the white. Both sexes of each of the eared pheasants look the same.

Nineteen of the forty nine pheasant species are in danger of extinction, due mainly to destruction of their forest habitats. In 1975 the World Pheasant Association was formed to help these endangerd birds, by working closely with the governments concerned and creating 140 reserves where the interests of the pheasants would be paramount. In Edinburgh Zoo, as in most zoos and private collections, the pheasants' eggs are taken away and incubated artificially, in order to ensure the maximum success rate.

MAP LOCATION 9   MAP LOCATION 46

Parrots

There are over 300 species in the family of birds known as the parrots. They include the parrots and parrakeets, the macaws and conures, the cockatoos and cockatiels, the lories and lorikeets, the lovebirds and, of course, the budgerigars. Basically, they are birds of the tropics, inhabiting parts of Africa, Asia, the Americas and Australasia. Many are brightly coloured and, generally, they are raucous. Several are particularly good mimics, which is one of the reasons why the demands of the pet trade have helped to decimate their populations. This fact, together with deforestation of their habitats, is responsible for the rare and endangered status of many species.

The Zoo is specialising in parrots and is liaising with other zoos to establish viable breeding pairs. Housed in the original Parrot Garden and in the south-facing aviaries of the Bird House, our birds represent only a few species and, where possible, we have more than one pair of each.

American Parrots

Our first breeding success has been with the green-winged macaw and the yellow-headed Amazon parrot (left). The eggs were incubated artificially and the birds handreared.

Other South American parrots with which we are working, are blue and yellow macaws (above left), yellow-naped macaws, severe macaws(far left), black-headed conures and red-lored Amazon parrots. Particularly attractive are our pairs of crimson and green thick-billed parrots (left) from Mexico.

Parrots are easily recognisable by their deep, strong beaks, ideally suited for cracking hard seeds and nuts, and often used as a third "foot" when climbing up tree trunks. Their feet have two toes pointing forwards and two backwards – an adaptation for tree climbing, and also, for manipulating their food.

MAP LOCATION 30   MAP LOCATION 31

Australasian Parrots

Parrots from this region are represented in Edinburgh Zoo by the well-known sulphur-crested cockatoo, a popular pet and good talker, the little corella cockatoo and the Molluccan cockatoo (right). Also on exhibit are Regent's parrots (below right), a group of little red-rumped parrakeets, plus cockatiels and budgerigars, which have bred readily in captivity for years.

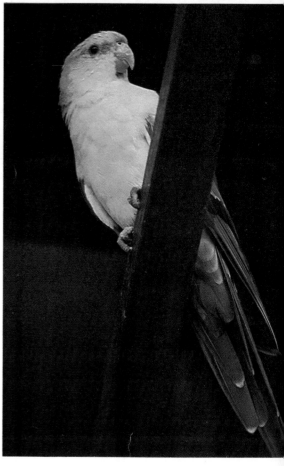

One of our most unusual parrots is the kea or mountain parrot (above) from New Zealand. This bird is sombre-coloured and camouflaged, apart from the undersides of its wings, which are a bright geranium hue, possibly for recognition by members of its own species. This is the only parrot to eat flesh, as a supplement to its vegetarian diet. Keas have long, curved beaks to enable them to uproot tubers and other vegetation from the ground.

MAP LOCATION 30   MAP LOCATION 31

Other Parrots

We are breeding ring-necked parrakeets from Asia and hope soon to breed the African grey parrot.

Usually no single specimens are kept in the Zoo – all our birds are in breeding pairs or groups, with suitable nesting facilities and accommodation provided.

Other than parrots and pheasants, the Zoo exhibits three further species of tropical bird, two of which are breeding regularly.

Rothschild's Mynah

This highly endangered bird exists only on the tiny island of Bali. In conjunction with Jersey Zoo we are making an excellent contribution to the captive breeding programmes of this species.

White-Cheeked Touraco

One of several species of touraco, this very beautiful African forest bird has bred several times in Edinburgh Zoo, all the chicks being parent-reared.

Red-Billed Hornbill

As yet we have not succeeded in breeding the hornbill. If our birds were to breed, the female would be "holed-up" in a hollow log by the male and he would feed her through a tiny aperture during the incubation of the eggs.

Wildfowl and Water Birds

Ducks, swans and geese are known as wildfowl and sometimes flamingoes are included in this group of birds. These and other birds associated with water, including storks, cranes, pelicans and ibises, inhabit the world's wetlands and are found in all continents. Many of them migrate seasonally to utilise food sources in different areas. Man's continual reclamation of wetlands for farming and development, and his pollution of the waterways, have seriously affected the populations of these birds.

The Duck Ponds

A variety of ducks, a number of geese and a pair of whooper swans are current residents on the Duck Ponds. These ponds, constructed in the early days of the Zoo, are scheduled for redevelopment and complete re-landscaping.

The ducks look their best in winter and spring, when in their breeding plumage. The males are brightly coloured to attract their mates: being ground nesters, the females are camouflaged to protect their eggs and chicks. Our ducks are pinioned so cannot fly out of the enclosure. Some of them breed, but the young often fall prey to the free-flying colony of night herons, or to stoats and weasels. The night herons were once captive but, when a storm damaged their aviary in the 1950s, they escaped but continue to live and breed in the trees round the Duck Ponds area. Resident ducks include mallards, common shelducks, pintails, widgeon, tufted ducks and mandarins.

Geese

Geese have strong, webbed feet, set well back on the body, and dense, waterproofed feathers, typical of this group of birds. As well as finding food in water, they graze on grasses and other plants. Red-breasted geese, Canada geese, barnacle geese (left) and greylags are represented in the Zoo.

Swans

The grace and beauty of swans have long been an inspiration to man in the fields of dance, music and art. Whooper swans, nesting in Iceland, often travel over 1000 miles to overwinter in Britain. Our stately pair of whooper swans (below), dominating the Duck Ponds, are a great attraction for visitors.

A single Australian black swan is at present exhibited with our pelicans. We hope to acquire a mate for it very soon.

Chilean Flamingo

Six species of flamingo are recognised and Edinburgh Zoo has a small breeding colony of the pale pink Chilean variety. Flamingoes usually breed in captivity only if kept in large numbers, so we are most encouraged by our success with relatively few birds.

They feed in lakes by straining tiny crustaceans and algae through a brush-like filter within their beaks, their tongues pumping the water through the sieve. In captivity, they lose their pink colouring unless the pigment carotin is added to their diet.

Their nests resemble "sand castles" made of mud, with a depression on the top to hold the single egg. Chicks have grey plumage for the first two years of life.

87

European White Stork ▼

One of the best-known storks, the white stork of Europe is considered to be a harbinger of good luck and the "bringer of babies" so far as some young children are concerned! Unlike cranes, storks nest high in trees, and have adapted to building nests on chimney pots and rooftops in some European countries. Sadly, they seldom do this today as their food sources outside the villages and towns are much depleted. Storks migrate annually to Africa and the Middle East.

Edinburgh Zoo keeps three white storks which have shown interest in nest-building, but have, so far, laid no eggs. The characteristic beak "clattering" is performed as a greeting or, depending on the body posture, as a warning to intruders.

MAP LOCATION 5

Wattled Crane ▲

Cranes only superficially resemble storks – they are not related to each other and have many physical and behavioural differences. Three of the fourteen species of crane are among the rarest birds in the world. Cranes are ground nesters and usually pair for life – in some parts of the world they are seen as symbols of loyalty. Their loud, trumpeting calls, often hauntingly beautiful, and graceful ritualised "dancing" are usually associated with courtship, but can be heard and seen at other times.

The rare wattled crane from Africa is endangered in the wild. It was hoped that the Zoo's young pair would breed but, tragically, the female died of shock, after breaking her leg and, at the time of going to press, we are still trying to locate another mate for our male.

MAP LOCATION 35

Waldrapp Ibis ▶

Of the several species of ibis, probably the one with which the majority of people are most familiar is the black and white sacred ibis. The Waldrapp ibis, once quite widespread in Europe, is now exceedingly rare and is confined to two small colonies – one in Turkey and the other in Morocco. A captive breeding programme was started in Basle Zoo with the eventual aim of releasing birds back into the wild in Switzerland.

Our birds are from the breeding group at Jersey Zoo and are housed in a specially designed aviary. We are involved both with Jersey Zoo and with Rabat Zoo in Morocco, in the management of this endangered bird. We managed to hand-rear five chicks in 1987 and these are now all in Chester Zoo. Hopefully our birds will rear their own chicks in 1988.

(MAP 1 LOCATION)

American White Pelican

Strong swimmers, due to their huge, paddle-shaped feet, and graceful fliers, despite their large bodies and beaks, pelicans occur in many parts of the world. Swimming in a horse-shoe formation, called a raft, pelicans drive shoals of fish ahead of them and dip their heads into the water simultaneously, scooping up the fish in the greatly distensible lower section of the beak.

In this species, a horny crest grows along the top of the bill in the breeding season.

(MAP 11 LOCATION)

Reptiles

Tortoises and turtles, lizards, snakes and crocodiles are all reptiles. Reptiles have a dry, scaly skin and all lay shelled eggs on land, even marine turtles, which spend their entire lives at sea. Reptiles are cold-blooded, which means that their body temperature is dependent on that of their surroundings. As a result, most reptiles live in the warmer parts of the world. A few that live in temperate zones retain their eggs inside the body, where they hatch and the young appear to be born "live".

The policy at Edinburgh Zoo is to keep a limited number of species and to put all our efforts into maintaining breeding groups of these, producing second to third generation captive-born reptiles where possible. As a result, some of our exhibits contain the same reptiles, but at different stages of growth. Several of our reptile breeding projects involve the Jersey Wildlife Preservation Trust.

Eggs laid in the Reptile House are usually removed to the off-exhibit Breeding Unit, where they are kept in incubators, with temperature and humidity closely monitored. This greatly improves the chances of the eggs hatching successfully.

Edinburgh Zoo keeps neither venomous snakes nor large crocodilians.

Lizards

Excellent breeding results have been achieved with the Chinese water dragon, the Australian bearded dragon (right), the leopard gecko, the plumed basilisk (above) and the blue-tongued skink. The latter hatches the eggs inside the body and gives birth to "live" young.

With the knowledge and experience gained from regular hatchings, we are now attempting to establish breeding groups of Australian water dragons, Hardwick's lizards, granite spiny lizards, and pink-tongued skinks (far left).

Our exhibits often contain both ground living and tree climbing lizards, in addition to tortoises or terrapins. This allows us to utilise all the exhibit space.

Snakes

Over the years we have often bred African pythons (page 90) and boa constrictors, and sometimes the eggs are left with the snakes for incubation. The boas retain the eggs within the body and can produce as many as 40 "live" young. More recently we have started to breed the false water cobra – so called because it mimics the highly venomous Indian cobra, the rainbow boa and the corn snake (left). We also exhibit Honduran milk snakes which, at present, are too young to breed.

Tortoises and Terrapins

In September 1987 we had our first hatching of Hermann's tortoise (right), the type of tortoise usually kept as pets until a few years ago. This species rarely bred in captivity and is now seriously endangered in the wild, due to the demands of the pet trade. We hope to breed red-footed tortoises from the West Indies in the near future.

Terrapins are often mixed with our other reptiles, and we have bred the side-necked terrapin and the European pond terrapin.

Crocodiles

Edinburgh Zoo no longer exhibits the large Nile crocodile or the Mississippi alligator – our accommodation is far too confined for these species and we could never have bred them. We now concentrate on the endangered dwarf crocodile from West Africa. Twice we have had fertile eggs from our pair, but, as yet, no successful hatchings. Considering our record with other reptiles, we hope the crocodiles will not defeat us for much longer. The nesting area in the exhibit is unavoidably untidy due to the activities of the crocodiles.

During the summer months, visitors may watch a video on reptile breeding and see incubating eggs in a viewing window of the Breeding Unit. Directions for how to get there are on display in the Reptile House.

MAP LOCATION 30

Amphibians

Frogs, toads, newts and salamanders are all amphibians. Like the reptiles, they are cold-blooded but, unlike the reptiles, they have damp, naked skins. The eggs of most species are laid in water, where they hatch into tadpoles. A few others lay their eggs in moist conditions, in the centre of plants where water collects or in "balls" of foam on the undersides of leaves – such adaptations occur only in tropical forests where conditions are extremely humid. Some amphibians are adapted to a life in trees.

Frogs

Several species of frog are exhibited in the Reptile House and, as with the reptiles, great efforts have been made to establish breeding colonies. Eggs are immediately removed to the Breeding Unit, where conditions for hatching can be provided and they can be closely monitored.

In 1986 we bred, for the first time, the red-eyed tree frog (above right) and the poison arrow frog, both from Costa Rica. The former is unusual in that the eggs are laid on foliage overhanging water so that the hatching tadpoles drop into the pool below, and the latter lays eggs on leaves on the forest floor, the male carrying water to them for their development.

We hope to breed soon Trinidadian stream frogs, tomato frogs, golden mantella frogs and White's tree frog (above left) from Australia.

Behind The Scenes

The role of the Zoo's Animal Department has changed somewhat over recent years. None of the breeding programmes you have read about would be possible without good zoo keepers. Zoo keeping, these days, is a profession, not merely a matter of feeding animals and cleaning out their stalls.

Many of our keepers have a sound knowledge of zoology and animal behaviour, and all new keepers must agree to enrol for the two-year Animal Management Course, now taught in all Federation zoos.

Today, great emphasis is placed on animal observation and written reports, and the keeping of accurate animal records is essential. Identification of individuals is also of paramount importance, especially with many animals going or arriving on breeding loan. Ear tags, leg rings and flipper bands indicate sex, year of birth, etc. Much off-exhibit work is done, particularly with artificial incubation of bird and reptile eggs, and hand-rearing of birds.

Diets are scientifically worked out and adhered to and animal foodstuff is of the highest quality. We ask you not to feed the animals as unsuitable food can actually harm them.

Edinburgh Zoo is fortunate in having the services of the Edinburgh University Veterinary Department, and members of the Large Animal Practice Teaching Unit visit the Zoo every week.

The Gorilla GP

*David Taylor, renowned Zoo vet and author of **One by One** and **The Zoo in You** series, gives some guidelines on how to survive as a Gorilla GP.*

Do elephants get toothache? Do parrots grumble about gout? Yes, they do. Gorillas and gnus, cheetahs and chipmunks – and all the rest of the over 2 million species of living creatures on earth – can sometimes, just like us, need a day in bed or a doctor's note.

The zoo vet's life is certainly a kaleidoscope. A medical doctor need only concentrate on one kind of patient, the vet who attends to your cat or dog sees perhaps six or seven animal species routinely, but the vets who take care of the Edinburgh Zoo have around 1200 different varieties of patient, each with its own peculiarities.

Of course you might imagine that <u>some</u> wild animals could be expected to

present medical problems more or less the same as those of their domesticated relatives. Can't zebras be regarded as just a sort of horse – liable to horsey ailments? To a certain extent, yes they can. Zebras do sometimes get colic and laminitis just like your pony, though far less frequently, and lions and tigers must be inoculated against ordinary cat flu and feline enteritis to stop them picking up bugs from any prowling cousins. But such similarities can be taken only so far; cheetahs are cats but they have their own unique and deadly form of liver disease. And anyway what domestic comparisons can be made with animals such as the elephant or dolphin? That's the problem. Many species of zoo animal have bodies that are designed and which function in ways far removed from those of familiar pet and farmyard beasts.

A zoo vet's patients, of course, differ from those of his medical and veterinary colleagues in one very important aspect; many of them are wild and dangerous and disinclined to let him stick an arm down their mouth or a stethoscope on their chest at the best of times, let alone when they have raging toothache or sport a grapefruit-sized boil on their bottom. One of the greatest advances in zoo medicine was made around 30 years ago when it first became possible to deliver tranquillisers or anaesthetics (or any other drug or vaccine) to an animal safely by means of an ingenious syringe that flies through the air. Accurate diagnosis and treatment of dangerous animals depends largely on these 'flying sleeping pills'. A whole range of specialized anaesthetics have been developed for exotic species, and with the aid of such wonderful chemicals, the zoo vet can quickly intervene to nip developing surgical and medical problems in the bud.

You might be surprised at the care and complexity of the health service that exists behind the scenes at Edinburgh and other great zoos. Dentistry, radiology, advanced laboratory tests on blood samples and other specimens, as well as abdominal and other surgery can all be handled efficiently. Many species are pampered with regular check-ups and much effort is put into preventive medicine – avoiding illness by supervising nutritional and vaccination programmes and generally

keeping each species' particular requirements for health and happiness to the fore.

The zoo vet is also deeply involved in the important conservation aspects of the zoo's life by studying the breeding and rearing of the animal stock. Artificial insemination, hormone therapy and now even embryo transplants are helping to secure the future for rare and endangered species. When babies are born there may be a host of infant problems to attend to; the chimp baby who must have his polio vaccine on a sugar lump just like a human child and the orphan baby seal that has to be reared on milk of a special kind made by blending herring and fish oil (cow's milk would kill it).

Every day I learn something new as a zoo vet; old friends and new additions to the zoo collections pose me fresh problems. It might be an eagle with fungus in its lungs or a young orang-utan spotty with measles. Whatever it is, it's a fascinating life and I wouldn't want to be anything other than a gorilla's G.P.

Education

In line with its charter and with the move, both national and international, for zoos to make a commitment to the education of their visitors, and of children in particular, the Royal Zoological Society of Scotland appointed its first Education Officer in 1971. A former cafeteria and souvenir shop were converted into an Education Centre, which was partly in operation from 1973 and was completed and officially opened by the Duke of Edinburgh, in 1976.

The Education Department now numbers fourteen staff, including teachers, graphic artists, secretary and technician. The Education Centre comprises three classrooms and a lecture theatre seating 220, in addition to offices and a library.

The department is funded by a grant from Lothian Regional Education Authority and by a nominal charge to Lothian Region pupils, using the service. Pupils from outside Lothian Region are charged at a higher rate.

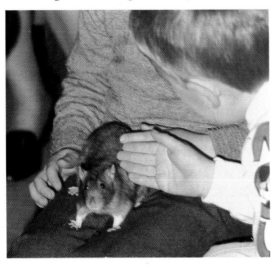

The Centre operates a comprehensive educational programme throughout the school year, offering a wide range of wildlife and conservation-based topics to school classes, from nursery through primary to secondary levels, and including those from special schools. All classes are taught by qualified instructors who also accompany the pupils to the relevant animals in the Park. In certain topics, live animals are used for contact and demonstration, and skulls, bones and skins are used where applicable. Activity sheets and teachers' notes are designed for all topics. In conjunction with a number of other organisations, including the Royal Museums of Scotland and the Royal Botanic Garden, the Education Department offers school classes (and adults) an educational project called "Interlink", whereby different aspects of a common theme are illustrated, on visits to the different organisations participating in a particular Interlink. Day and evening classes are available for adults, and specialist classes are arranged for college and university students.

The graphic artists are responsible for the design of all the Zoo's animal labels, in addition to that of our educational programmes and activity sheets.

In 1987, a further educational facility was added, with the opening of ZooLab – a multi-disciplinary "classroom" where school teachers can develop with their pupils, projects involving art and crafts, puppetry, mime and music,

and language, using the Zoo animals as their inspiration and resource. ZooLab is housed in the former Acclimatisation House and teachers using it must attend an in-service course run by the Zoo's Education Department.

Throughout the Easter and summer school holidays, and during weekends in May and June, educational activities for the general visitor are manned by the Society's team of adult and junior Volunteers. These activities include Animal Contact Sessions, a Brass Rubbing Centre and Information Stations.

Details of all current educational programmes are available from the Education Centre, Edinburgh Zoo, Murrayfield, Edinburgh EH12 6TS, Telephone 031-334 9171.

The Royal Zoological Society of Scotland

The Royal Zoological Society of Scotland (RZSS) is a charitable, non-profitmaking organisation devoted to the study and conservation of wildlife. It was founded in 1909 to promote a greater knowledge of animal life among the Scottish people. Today, it is one of the nation's foremost conservation organisations, owning both Edinburgh Zoo and the Highland Wildlife Park. These unique and exciting animal collections form the Scottish National Zoological Collection.

Membership

Membership of the Royal Zoological Society of Scotland is open to everyone and can cost as little as 3p a day. Members are entitled to unlimited free entry to Edinburgh Zoo and the Highland Wildlife Park. Other benefits include discounted entry for Members' guests, a year round programme of events and exclusive use of Edinburgh Zoo's Members' House which boasts a

first class restaurant, cocktail bar, comfortable lounges and conference suites. In addition younger members can join the Gannet Club which meets on eight Saturdays a year to undertake a wide variety of activities related to nature and wildlife.

Membership forms are available throughout the Park or by writing to the Membership Secretary.

Volunteers

The Society has over 100 adult and junior volunteers who assist the permanent staff in a variety of spheres including manning the shops and Brass Rubbing Centre, conducting Animal Handling classes, and staffing information stations and gardening.

Volunteers are given a course of training and familiarisation sessions, and a name badge. The volunteer scheme is operated by the Zoo's Education

Department and all our volunteers are members of the Society. If you are interested or would like further details, contact the Education Centre.

Species Support

The Species Support Scheme allows individuals and organisations to actively assist the Society by paying their chosen animal's annual food bill. All the animals at Edinburgh Zoo and the Highland Wildlife Park are available for sponsorship and fees range from as little as £10. Species Supporters in return receive a certificate, the scheme's quarterly newsletter, *Ark File*, and if the annual support fee amounts to £50 or more, a specially engraved plaque is affixed to their animal's enclosure. The Species Support Scheme is a wonderful

means of showing that you care about wildlife. For further details please write to the Species Support Secretary.

Further details can be obtained from: The Royal Zoological Society of Scotland, Murrayfield, Edinburgh EH12 6TS, Telephone 031 334 9171.

Where to Tomorrow?

Nothing stands still in the zoo world and from the moment this guide book goes to press, there will be changes occurring in several spheres within Edinburgh Zoo.

The sounds of cement mixers, dumper trucks, welding and stone chipping have, over the last few years, become as familiar in the Zoo as the calls of the penguins and the barking of the sea lions. Hopefully, our visitors notice the fruits of all this labour – our policy of continuous improvement within the Park. The early summer of 1988 should see the completion of the Rock Dens, the Small Carnivore Complex and the Coati Exhibit – all projects sponsored by the Manpower Services Commission.

The major development of 1988 and early 1989 will be the Orientation Centre, together with the new Entrance and Zoo Shop. Her Majesty The Queen is due to open the Orientation Centre on 30 June 1988 –

a great honour for us in this our 75th Anniversary Year. The construction of the Entrance and Zoo Shop will follow. The Orientation Centre is intended to help visitors get the most out of their time in the Zoo and, in addition to familiarising everyone with up-to-date information, it will house an exciting exhibition on the role of zoos today. The new Entrance will facilitate entry, both from the road and car park, and will be designed in such a way that queues are minimised. The proposed Zoo Shop will have much more space for the display of a wider range of merchandise and will be accessible to members of the public who are not actually visiting the Zoo.

Priority will then be given to the upgrading and extending of the main Penguin Exhibit which, these days, does not do justice to our achievements in breeding the birds. Other enclosures due to be redesigned are the Duck Ponds, the Cassowary Pens and the Polar Bear Pool – an assurance that the cement mixers and dumper trucks will be with us for some time yet!

Since the bird pages of this book went to press, we have acquired the only pair of single-wattled cassowaries in Britain. This species occurs in New Guinea and we hope very much to be able to repeat with them, the success we achieved in the breeding of our Australian cassowaries. Also too late to be mentioned in the bird pages, was the safe hatching of Edinburgh Zoo's first kea chicks (the parents are referred to on page 84).

There are no imminent plans to bring new species into the collection, other than those already mentioned in the text. Our efforts will be concentrated both on maintaining the excellent breeding success rate we have already established with a very high percentage of our mammals, and on solving the problems regarding those that continue to defeat us, including the gorillas,

cheetahs and snow leopards. We fully expect to breed some of the more recent arrivals, such as the Persian leopards, bush dogs, coatis and, possibly, the otters. Considerable advances have been made in Edinburgh Zoo in the last few years, with birds, but we hope for further breakthrough with more of our parrots and owls, and, with luck, the golden eagles. Breeding in the Reptile House goes from strength to strength, but safely-hatched crocodiles would be the ultimate triumph.

Great emphasis will continue to be placed on our contribution to the Operation Scimitar Oryx project and more of our herd's progeny will, hopefully, be reintroduced to their countries of origin. Should our support be required in other viable reintroduction programmes, concerning animals which breed well here, it will be readily offered.

Edinburgh Zoo aims to become an exemplary model of conservation in action, where staff dedication and modern technology combine to form a highly professional organisation, involved and co-operating internation-ally to help hold at bay, man's mass destruction of his fellow creatures.

The Highland Wildlife Park

The Highland Wildlife Park at Kincraig, near Kingussie, was opened in 1972 with the objective of displaying a collection of Scotland's animals and plants in their natural setting. In doing so it aims to promote a knowledge and understanding of these most beautiful animals so that people may appreciate the vital role they have played, and continue to play, in the landscape and customs of the Scottish Highlands.

The Park is unlike any zoo or safari park – it takes you back to a time before man's invasion of Scotland in 6,000 BC, when wolves, bears, lynx, wild boar and wild horses roamed wild and free in Scotland. At the Wildlife Park they can still be seen in 250 acres of stunningly beautiful Scottish countryside, alongside many typical Scottish animals, such as red grouse and wildcats.

The Park combines a large drive-through area in which grazing animals

can be viewed from the comfort of your car and a walk-through area containing smaller animals in natural, spacious enclosures and aviaries. There is an attractive cafeteria, gift shop, exhibition area and pets corner. The Park is open from March – October. It is situated between Aviemore and Kingussie on the B9152, leaflets are available from the Zoo Shop.

The Highland Wildlife Park has been owned by the Royal Zoological Society of Scotland since 1986. Members of the Society have free entry to the Park.

IT'S ELECTRIC

A fraction over 12 seconds – that's all it takes to enjoy the pleasures of open air motoring in the new XJ-S V12 Convertible.

At the touch of a button, the hood folds back and the heated glass rear window is stowed automatically out of sight.

Out on the open road, the 5.3 litre engine gives an effortless performance which is complemented by an advanced anti-lock braking system like no other in the world. Developed by a team of engineering perfectionists, it even has anti-yaw control.

While to keep you firmly in your place are body-hugging, heated sports seats, upholstered in leather.

The new XJ-S V12 Convertible – a driving experience not to be missed.

Call in today to arrange your test drive.

Appleyard Jaguar

107 Glasgow Road, Edinburgh EH12 8LH
Telephone: 031-334 9753

TOGETHER WE'RE A BREED APART

JAGUAR

THE NEW V12 CONVERTIBLE XJS

WORLD SPORTSCAR CHAMPIONS

Index

71,256,581

Seventy-one million, two hundred and fifty-six thousand, five hundred and eighty-one teeth meltingly delicious rashers of bacon.

Last year, we produced enough bacon rashers to ensure that the population never had to go without their traditional breakfast.

More than enough to start the day the bacon and egg way.

And still leave an ample sufficiency for snacks, fetes, teas and picnics; bean-feasts, elevenses, lunches and dinners.

Seventy million rashers of Halls bacon were eaten by bacon lovers all over the country who passionately believe we're the best.

We know we are.

IT HAS TO BE

HALL'S

BRITISH FOOD Quality

Contact: David A Hall Ltd, Broxburn. Bacon curers. Suppliers of sausage, pies, cooked meats and delicatessen products. Telephone: 0506 853300. Telex: 727062 PORKIE G.

LAURISTON CASTLE

A late-16th century tower-house with extensive 19th century additions, the castle stands in attractive grounds overlooking the Firth of Forth. In the interior it is preserved as an Edwardian upper-class country mansion. It contains period and reproduction furniture and impressive collections of Derbyshire Blue John, Crossley wool mosaics and objets d'art. There is a free car park. Visitors are given a guided tour of about 40 minutes duration.

OPEN

April to October, Daily (except Friday) 11am-1pm, 2-5pm (last tour begins at approximately 4.20pm) November to March, Saturdays and Sundays only 2-4pm (last tour begins at approximately 3.20pm). Telephone 031-336 2060.

ADMISSION CHARGES

Adults: 80p. Children: O.A.P's, UB40's and Benefit Recipients. 40p. Admission to the grounds is free.

DAVIDSON'S MAINS, EDINBURGH

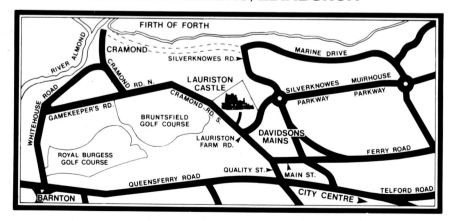

THE MILLER GROUP LTD

CONSTRUCTION · DEVELOPMENTS · HOMES · MINING

Miller House, 18 South Groathill Avenue, Edinburgh EH4 2LW
Telephone 031-332 2585. Telex 727551 MILCON G. Fax 031-332 3426.

Regional Offices at: London, Glasgow, Altrincham, Godalming, Newton Mearns, Normanton, Rugby, Stockton, Wakefield, Winchester, Indiana U.S.A.

A SCOTTISH LANDMARK · WORLD·WIDE!

The attractions of
E D I N B U R G H
Scotland's Capital City

Within the natural scenic beauty and architectural splendour of its old and new towns, Edinburgh offers a rich variety of entertainment and fascinating places to visit. It boasts some of the finest museums and galleries, the International Festival and a full programme of dance and drama throughout the year. Featured here are some of the unique visitor attractions that make Edinburgh one of the most exciting cities in the world.

EDINBURGH *WAX* MUSEUM

Presents Scottish History in Wax. Three Floors of Sheer Enchantment Children (of all ages) will love 'Never Never Land' and visit (if you dare) 'The Chamber of Horrors'. See our new Space Ship with E.T., Mr. Spock, Luke Skywalker & Princess Leah. Open seven days a week – Special Group Rates.

142 High Street, Edinburgh. Tel: 031 226 4445

EDINBURGH *MILITARY* TATTOO

Throughout the Festival in August, Edinburgh's ancient castle is the setting for the world's best-known and best-loved military spectacle – The Edinburgh Military Tattoo. This vast international event draws audiences and performers from all over the world to enjoy, as the sun goes down across the esplanade, pipers, bands and displays of skill and daring. An unrivalled pageant of Scotland's history and tradition.

Details available after December each year from: The Tattoo Office, 22 Market Street, Edinburgh EH1 1QB Tel: 031 225 1188.

THE SCOTCH *WHISKY* HERITAGE CENTRE

This major new tourist attraction is next to Edinburgh Castle Esplanade. Academically researched, the history of the whisky industry will be depicted by audio-visual presentation, a working model of a distillery, life size figures in theatrical sets with appropriate sound effects and aromas. Take a seat in an electric barrel car, journey back in time and learn something of the mystique of the Scotch Whisky Industry. A visit will take approximately one hour.

The Scotch Whisky Heritage Centre, 358 Castlehill, The Royal Mile, Edinburgh EH1 2NE. Tel: 031 220 0441. Open 7 days a week from 9.00am.

GHOSTS *AND* GHOULS

Edinburgh's Premier Horror Walk. A terrifying guided walk to scenes of macabre murder, phantom phenomena and vicious vengeance!
Be enthralled by authentic tales of Edinburgh's bloodcurdling past. Afterwards revive your spirits in a local tavern.... the gruesome tales continue into the night.
Leave at 8pm every night from May 1 to Sept 30 from Edinburgh's ancient meeting spot – the Mercat Cross beside St Giles in the Royal Mile.

Party bookings for offices, schools etc available all year round.
Bookings/Enquiries Tel: 031 661 4541.

EDINBURGH *ZOO*

Edinburgh Zoo is Scotland's largest and most exciting animal collection with over 200 species of wild animals in 80 acres of hillside parkland. World famous for its penguin colony and unique daily penguin parade at 2.30pm in Summer. A new visitor centre opens in July 1988 and children's activity area, restaurants, bars and a shop make it the complete day out for all ages.
Open daily all year 9am to 6pm or dusk.

Edinburgh Zoo, Corstorphine Road, Edinburgh EH12 6TS. Tel: 031 334 9171.

DISCOVER *HISTORIC* SCOTLAND

Visit Scotland's most famous castle, Edinburgh, and discover Edinburgh's other historic castle – Craigmillar – where the death of Mary Queen of Scots' second husband, Lord Darnley, was plotted in 1566. 2½ miles S.E. of the City Centre on the A68.

For further details on these and other historic sites contact your Local Information Centre or,

HISTORIC SCOTLAND

Historic Buildings and Monuments, 20 Brandon Street, Edinburgh EH3 5RA. Tel: 031 244 3101 Mon – Fri. 9 am – 5 pm.

GREAT BEERS, GREAT SERVICE.

ALLOA

« C O M I N G   R I G H T   U P »